Write
Nonfiction
NOW!

GUIDE TO
WRITING
AND
PUBLISHING
ARTICLES

REVISED AND EXPANDED

NINA AMIR

P5C
PURE SPIRIT
CREATIONS

Published 2025 by Pure Spirit Creations

www.purespiritcreations.com
Placitas, NM

Ordering Information:
Special discounts are available on quantity purchases
by corporations, associations, and others.
For details, contact nina@ninaamir.com.

Layout and Design by Shabbir Hussain Badshah.

Cover Design by Daniel Eyenegho.

Author photo by Rick Rood.

The Write Nonfiction NOW!
Guide to Writing and Publishing Articles
Revised and Expanded/Nina Amir—3rd ed.

ISBN (paperback): 978-0-9835353-9-3

Table of Contents

INTRODUCTION

Articles Are Nonfiction, Too!

By Nina Amir

Most people think of me as a nonfiction author and author coach or as the Inspiration to Creation Coach. I'm also a Transformational Coach and Certified High Performance Coach™. However, I began my publishing career as a magazine journalist.

I still love writing articles, and I use my journalistic skills as often as possible. I love to query magazines with ideas and receive and complete assignments. I enjoy conducting interviews and taking the information I've compiled and putting it together into a cohesive and interesting article. And of course, I enjoy seeing my words in print, not just on my computer screen but in a glossy publication.

Writing articles, which are nonfiction prose that comprise an independent part of a magazine or newspaper, can be a satisfying career but also provides a fabulous training ground for becoming a nonfiction author. My college professor, the late John Keats, once told me that if I could write a magazine article, I could write a book. After all, he claimed, a nonfiction book is just a collection of articles on one topic organized and bound together.

He was right.

As a young girl, I knew I wanted to be a writer. In fact, I wanted to write fiction. (Imagine that!) When I shared my dream with my mother, she said, "Only really good writers can make a living as novelists."

I interpreted that to mean I was *not* such a writer. I could have gone into therapy to heal this emotional wound, but I'm a take-action sort of person. Instead, I enrolled in a high school journalism class and soon discovered I loved writing articles. I also learned that I could eek out a living as a journalist. I liked magazines and began to dream of working for a big publication in New York City writing self-help articles.

I began my journalism career in high school, racking up bylines in local print publications. Many experts tell you not to write for free, and I'd agree—if possible. I admit, though, that I began writing without pay. My first bylines were earned writing a bi-weekly school news column for the local paper in my town. I progressed to the county paper and to another local paper. In college I wrote for the campus newspaper and magazine. I also interned every summer for newspapers. These initial free assignments and jobs gave me enough "clips" to gain paid assignments and a job upon graduation.

After college, I landed a paid full-time writing and editing job. However, I gave up my dream of working for a New York City glossy magazine when I discovered my first job at *Self* or *Glamour* had to be as a receptionist. After four years of learning to write and edit at a top-notch journalism school, I wasn't willing to answer phones.

I also learned that once past the receptionist level, most jobs for young staff were in editorial. I had received editorial training in college, and it served me well (and still does when I am hired for nonfiction book editing projects). But I wanted to write. So, I applied to small, regional magazines, and landed a job writing and editing.

My first two magazine jobs were located immediately outside of New York City in Westchester County. In addition to using my editing skills, I wrote both short and long articles for the magazines, garnering some nice bylines during those first few years. I also wrote freelance pieces for other regional publications.

I went on to work in the communication department for a large corporation in Manhattan, where I did more editing and writing as well as design work. After that, I took a job in Oklahoma for a consultant that, again, involved editing, writing, and design. These jobs afforded me many more bylines and lots of experience.

I then struck out on my own, opening a freelance writing company in Atlanta, GA. I began to freelance full-time as a writer and an editor—books, articles, essays, ads, newsletters—any work I could find. Much later, after editing a number of books, a few of which went on to become quite successful, I started writing my own nonfiction books. But my ability to write articles helped me conceptualize and complete those manuscripts.

I still love to write for publication. There's nothing like writing an essay or article, submitting it to a magazine or newspaper, and then opening up that publication to find your story published there—hopefully verbatim—with your byline showing off the fact that you composed every one of those words.

And to get paid for doing what you love . . . well, that's even better.

There are so many different types of articles to choose from. Profiles, news stories, trend pieces, human-interest articles, personal essays, and opinion pieces—take your pick. Depending upon what you like to write about, you can find one or two article forms you enjoy using and numerous magazines, newspapers, trade journals, or e-zines happy to publish your work.

As long as you don't fictionalize the content, you are writing nonfiction. (If you choose to write personal essays, remember that.)

Articles are a form of nonfiction and a fulfilling and profitable way to make a living as a writer—and to pursue your interests. In journalism school, we had to choose a concentration in addition to our major. The reason given was simple: It's helpful if a journalist has an area of expertise or subject about which they write often. (I write about choosing a niche later in this book).

I chose psychology. This area of expertise helped me produce the self-help articles I dreamed of writing. Later, it supported my desire to write about personal development. More than that, this educational focus gave me a credential, or the authority, to write for a particular niche.

What do you enjoy writing about? What are your passions and interests? What experience or knowledge do you posses? These subjects or interest areas, along with your life experience, make great fodder for articles and essays—written work someone will pay you to produce.

As my nonfiction writing blog (writenonfictionnow.com) encourages: Write Nonfiction *Now!* And, as the tagline on my main website (ninaamir.com) indicates, Achieve More Inspired Results by writing articles!

WHY WRITE FOR PUBLICATION

Earn a Living with Your Words

By Nina Amir

Create a career as a writer and earn a living with your words. As a nonfiction writer, it's possible to make this dream a reality.

Although most authors—nonfiction or fiction—don't make enough from book sales to pay their rent or mortgage, as a nonfiction writer, you have a multitude of options for getting paid for your writing. In fact, you can have a lucrative writing career if you are willing to branch out and write for different types of publications, markets, or clients. If you also have the ability to write about a variety of topics, and do so professionally, you can become a busy and well-paid writer.

Consider the following opportunities.

Write Articles and Essays

You can write articles or essays and get paid well for them. Despite the news about the death of print magazines and newspapers, many publications remain alive and well—and in need of freelance writers. Regional magazines and newspapers may pay on the low end of the scale ($25-$250 per piece), but mass-market publications can pay handsomely ($1-$2 per word).

Write for Businesses and Organizations

Business writing is the most lucrative way to make a living as a writer. If you have ever worked for a corporation, organization, or small business, you may have the experience necessary to land yourself some high-paying work. However, if you have marketing savvy and can write well, you can break into this market. You can write blog posts, white papers, marketing materials, ebooks, direct response letters, newsletters, and more. To break in, you just need to land one client. His or her testimonial will help you obtain your second client, and so on. For great information on how to get started in this area, check out thewellfedwriter.com.

Write for Websites and Blogs

The advent of the Internet opened up a whole new market for professional writers. Now you can write for websites, blogs, and online publications. Most businesses have a website or a blog or both, and many need help producing content. Numerous print magazines have added online editions. Seek out and offer your services to websites and publications in your area of interest or expertise. Or simply promote your writing services to sites in need of a writer.

Repurpose Your Work into Books

If you have been writing for publication for a while, you can repurpose your work into books. Be sure you have only sold the first rights to your articles or blog posts. This gives you the ability to use previously published work in other ways—such as in ebooks.

Consider writing a series of articles for a local newspaper or a series of essays for a national magazine. Then compile them into a book manuscript, add a bit of new content, and you've got a product to sell.

To Specialize or Not to Specialize

A strong argument exists for developing a writing specialty. If you are an authority on a topic or have developed expertise by writing about a specific subject, you can land assignments more easily if they relate to this interest area. Editors may even seek you out.

However, if you want to obtain more work, it might behoove you to generalize. Then you can write for more publications because you have the ability to cover a wide variety of topics.

I often get approached by editors who know I write about boys who dance and personal development and spirituality. However, I've also written about celebrities, business, sports, and parenting.

No reason exists for you to pigeonhole yourself into one of the areas I've mentioned. You can choose to write for all of these markets—or just one. Either way you will find yourself earning a living from your words.

Should You Pursue a Career in Print Journalism?

The digital age has made it difficult for print publications to stay in business. Many publications have had to morph to say afloat, and that fact has given many a budding journalist reason to wonder if pursuing a career in print journalism still represents a wise choice. Those wanting to freelance as magazine or newspaper writers also sometimes pause to consider if querying traditional publications is a waste of time.

I believe you can still find many opportunities to write for both local and national publications. National magazines continue to have a budget for freelance articles in most cases, and community newspapers often rely on freelancers to provide stories.

That said, other magazines and newspapers have little or no budget for feature writers in addition to their staff. They may, however, have a small budget for short fillers, op eds or online articles. And once you have proven yourself as a reliable provider of articles, you might be able to finagle yourself into a larger article for pay.

Many print publications have totally transitioned into online, rather than printed, versions. These may have more money to pay freelancers because their overhead costs are less. Drop your idea of holding a printed publication with your by-lined article in it and become accustomed to "clipping" articles on the internet instead. You will actually find these much more useful for landing additional assignments; you can provide three to five links to your published work in your next query letter.

I have stacks of magazines everywhere and regularly bring home one for which I hope to write. I also read online publications. The better you know a publication, the higher the likelihood you will develop a winning article idea for that magazine or newspaper.

Don't let anyone tell you print publications are all are dead. Some have moved into cyberspace, but many are still alive and well in the physical world. And the editors might be quite happy to see your query letter come across their desks—and to pay you for your article.

Building Platform with Bylined Articles

By Nina Amir

Writing articles in your area of expertise builds platform for both aspiring authors and journalists. That platform helps you sell your work, which is the goal for any type of writer.

You can create a platform, which is most-easily defined as a built-in audience for your work, in a variety of ways, such as writing for publication, speaking, and social networking. Your involvement in these activities helps you develop visibility, reach, authority, and influence in your target market.

Aspiring authors need platform to sell books both to readers and publishers. Writers who want to work as journalists need platform to sell assignments to publications.

Every byline represents another "board" in your platform. Your published articles, especially in your area of expertise, become a body of work that clearly proves you can write and produce an authoritative piece targeted at a market and to a publication's specifications and deadlines. Additionally, they expose you to a broad audience, readers who may choose to seek you out in other places online and off. This means you gain fans and followers, media gigs, and new assignments for editors.

Today numerous ways exist to get bylines in both print and virtual publications—and to get paid for doing so.

Consider writing for:

1. regional magazines

2. national magazines

3. local newspapers

4. business publications

5. niche publications

6. corporate publications

7. university publications

8. organization publications

9. e-zines (online magazines)

10. blogs

You can even write for sites like Medium or Substack. (The latter offers a way for readers to pay you for your work.) Both options have a built-in audience willing to branch out and read—and follow—new writers to the site.

How do you get started? Simply begin querying publications with your ideas.

If you've never written for publication before, you may need to begin with local or online publications, rather than large magazines. Although you can offer "shorts" (short articles) to the mass-market publications to get in the door and established.

I'm not a big advocate of working for free, but doing so can be an easy way to get your first journalistic credits. If you aren't concerned about pay, or if you want to promote yourself or your other work (such as a nonfiction book), writing for blogs and online publications provides great exposure. Or try writing for small or regional print publications. Additionally, try writing for trade journals published on your area of expertise.

Writing essays offers another route to publication. A personal essay doesn't require you to do any research or interviews, nor does it have to be long. Your life experience is enough fodder to fill several pages, and you surely have much to say about what happens to you, why it happens to you, and what others can learn from what happens to you. Essays are great platform elements for those who plan to write memoir.

Or try writing opinion pieces as a way to get started. Many local newspapers still publish op ed articles, and you can make a name for yourself and get to know editors by becoming a reliable source of content. These opinion pieces can result in additional types of assignments.

Before you submit a query, research the publication and the type of articles they publish. Look for the publication's submission guidelines, and read them carefully. Then write a one-page query letter, and send it off. Rinse and repeat.

Don't forget that writing articles builds platform for nonfiction book authors and helps sell books as well. As I began to focus on books I planned to write and publish, I wrote articles for free and for pay and published them online in journals and publications where I could get exposure and links to my work. I also sold articles to a variety of print publications, purposely building platform and expert status on and off the internet in specific subject areas.

I use my journalism skills to build platform in other ways as well, including each time I promote myself on the Internet by posting news releases or social media updates.

While I get a lot of satisfaction out of writing an article that appears in good old-fashioned print media and for which I receive a big fat check, the platform I build by doing so serves my writing career in many other ways.

HOW TO GET STARTED
AS A JOURNALIST

The First Step Toward Becoming a Journalist

By Nina Amir

If you want to become a journalist, you must develop an idea you can pitch to a newspaper or magazine. That's how you get started.

To write for a newspaper, look for news stories about which the local newspaper might not be aware. Maybe you know a local organization having an event, your child is on a local team that is going to nationals, your neighborhood has had a rash of crime, or a local businessperson recently received an award. These represent great news stories to propose.

Regional magazines might be interested in the same topics if you can write a longer piece for a broader audience. Maybe you can profile the local businessperson and show how he has impacted the area in which he lives, for example. Or you could write about crime in the region.

National magazines, of course, need stories of interest to a national audience. Sometimes you can turn a local story into a national one. For instance, you could write a trend piece about the rise in crime in rural areas or about how people in certain communities are lowering crime rates by meditating.

Once you have a story idea, consider how you will approach it. Will you write in the first person or third? Will you interview experts? Will you include personal experience? What angle will you take? How will you target the market? How long will the piece be? Check the publication for which you plan to write to ensure the article you plan to write conforms to its requirements. Writers' guidelines for most publications can be found online.

Determine how to contact the publication. Most prefer an emailed query, but some local newspapers allow phone queries.

For a news story, query your local newspaper and ask if they are interested in the story and mention you would like to write the piece. If you have no bylines to your name, offer to write it on speculation (without pay until they accept it). Or offer to do the piece for free so you obtain that vital first byline. Or write the story and submit it on spec.

When you query a magazine, however, create an idea that does not involve news and therefore is not timebound. Unless you plan to write for a news magazine, most publications look for evergreen topics that can be run at any time of the year or articles related to themes, like summer, holidays, or issues that concern their readership or their magazine's special niche.

Once you have a strong and unique idea that targets the publication's market, craft a compelling query letter.

Now you're ready to send that letter and discover if you have landed your first assignment as a journalist.

How to Get Your First Article Byline

By Nina Amir

If you have never had an article published, you know that first gig can prove the most difficult one to land. On the other hand, if you have many bylines under your belt, you are aware that landing freelance writing assignments gets easier. Additionally, you are more likely to get paid something for most, if not all, of your work. So, how do you get that first byline, or more of them, so landing paid gigs becomes your norm?

How to Get Your First Byline

Some writers produce a few free articles for local newspapers when they first start out as journalists or professional writers. Many experts frown on this practice, though, believing writers should never write anything for free.

As I mentioned, I wrote many free articles as an intern while still in college to get those sought-after bylines that would help me get paid assignments (and a job) after graduation. Today, I still occasionally write articles for publications that provide me or my books with good "exposure." In other words, they provide promotional opportunities, build my platform, and enhance my expert status. I try most of the time to get paid for my work, though.

Of course, blogging entails writing for free, as does guest blogging. "Free" has become much more acceptable, especially if you are trying to build platform or promote your work. (And every aspiring or published author, as well as professional writer, should have a blog. It's the way your website gets discovered.)

If you want to earn a living as a writer, you do, indeed, want to get paid for your writing. I studied magazine journalism in college and was taught never to write an article unless I knew beforehand that I would get paid for it. I've tried to stick to this rule as much as possible—unless I'm consciously writing for free for reasons already mentioned.

Before you resign yourself to writing for free to get your first byline, here are some ways to get both credit and a paycheck for your work.

Write for Local or Regional Publications

Seek out some local or regional publications that might pay you even a modest sum for your work. Get those bylines—and paychecks—under your belt, and then approach the larger publications, such as national magazines, that pay more.

Start a Blog

Develop a "clip file" by starting your own blog. Build an archive of blog posts to show to publications in lieu of free article bylines ass you build a visibility and an expert platform online. You also can guest blog for other sites, some of which might pay for posts.

Create Your Own Online Column

Write for an organization like Huffpost.com. This allows you to get a small amount of pay at the same time as developing a platform with an online news service. You can direct editors to your articles there to prove you have the ability to write.

You also can create a column at Substack.com or Medium.com and get paid a bit of money. For instance, you can offer a paid version of your Substack, "newsletter" and subscribers pay to read this content.

Online Article and Content Services

There are a number of other places to write online and, in some cases, get paid. As you develop bylines with these services or sites, you can use them to land bigger and better freelance assignments. For instance, you could write for:

1. HubPages

2. Yahoo! Contributor Network

3. Dotdashmeredith.com

4. Wizzley

5. Listverse

6. Instantshift

Finding Other Freelance Work

Other places to search for freelance gigs of all types—and even some longer-term or full-term writing work—include:

1. journalismjobs.com

2. mediabistro.com

3. problogger.net

4. marketlist.com

5. Fiverr.com

6. Upwork.com

7. iwriter.com

8. wizzley.com

9. digitaljournal.com

10. constant-content.com

Even if you get a writing job from a site like upwork.com, you can use the finished project as a credit or byline. If your work appears online, direct an editor to that page to see an example of your work.

Look for national publications if you want bigger pay or regional, local, or niche publications if you are just starting out. However, some of the specialty publications that cater to profitable markets or wealthy audiences also pay quite well—even for newbie journalists or professional writers. This is especially true if you have an expertise in the subject area, so keep that in mind.

7 Ways to Get Your First Byline

By Nina Amir

Not every writer wants to write a book. Some want to earn their living as writers, and books aren't necessarily such a great way to accomplish that goal—unless you write a lot of bestsellers.

You can bring in a decent income by writing for publications, though. And, yes, there are still some publications out there willing to pay. In fact, in addition to traditional magazines and newspapers, you can write for a variety of online venues that also pay. Plus, you can produce content for businesses.

Of course, the big hurdle tends to be getting that first assignment and byline. How will you get it?

Let's look at some ways you can get your work published and possibly receive a paycheck for that work

1. **Submit shorts to magazines.** A great way to break into the magazine industry is with short articles. Most magazines have a section near the front of the publications where they run brief newsy pieces. These run 250-350 words. You may be able to write one off the top of your head or based on just a small amount of research, possibly from a small news bit you find somewhere that pertains to the publication's readership. Produce a few of these successfully, and the magazine might take you on for a longer article.

2. **Write op eds for your local newspaper.** Most newspapers need these opinion-based articles; thus, it tends to be an easier way to begin your publishing career. You may or may not get paid, but you will receive a byline. Write a few, and you'll have something to show an editor at a larger magazine or newspaper.

3. **Write for your local daily or weekly newspaper.** Often these papers are low on staff (and funds). They may be happy to take an article based on a local event but that they cannot send a reporter to cover. Consider writing about your daughter's swim team or your son's debate team. If a local author will be speaking at the library, ask if you can interview him for the paper. They may be thrilled to take your piece on speculation, which means they pay you and publish it if it meets their standards.

4. **Submit essays and articles to online publications.** Unfortunately, many online magazines do not pay. However, they have editors who make decisions about what to publish. Therefore, you can claim these published pieces as clips. It will go through an editorial review process and possibly even editing. Once posted online, it serves as a clip for you to show to other editors. And sometimes a few gigs with an online publication opens the door to writing for the print edition.

5. **Post your work on paid writing sites.** A variety of sites will take your work and reimburse you in some way. These include www.Yahoo.com, and www.Helium.com. (See the previous chapter, which provides a lengthy list of sites.) Some will check the quality of your work, others will not. Some editors will consider this work "bylined." At least you will be getting paid for your work, and you can direct editors to the links—and they will see your bylines.

6. **Contract yourself out as a copywriter.** In this case you may not have bylines per se to show. But you can get testimonials from your clients and provide these to an editor.

7. **Write for bloggers.** You can find paid blogging jobs. Your name may or may not appear on those blog sites, but if the owner of the blog verifies that you are the author of the posts, this might be enough to land you an assignment on a magazine or newspaper.

What Every Writer Needs to Know about Conducting an Interview

By Nina Amir

My journalism training included just a bit of information on how to conduct interviews. However, interviews represent an essential part of what I do as a journalist, a blogger, and an author. I use interviews every time I write an article that requires that I quote expert sources or write a book that requires research on a particular subject, especially if I choose to go directly to expert sources for information.

When you decide to write articles for publication, you increase the likelihood that you, too, will need to conduct interviews. If you've ever watched Diane Sawyer, Katie Couric, Howard Stern, Larry King, Oprah Winfrey, or Barbara Walters interview someone, you know there is an art to a good interview. Over the years I've learned a few tricks and rules myself.

Start with an "Overview" Source

First, if you are interviewing several sources for an article or a book project, it's best, if possible, to start with a source who can provide a general overview of your subject. With this information, you can begin to hone your questions to more specific ones. Direct these to sources with more specific knowledge. In fact, your first source may be able to supply contact information or suggestions for other expert sources.

Find Sources via Online Services

Second, if you are looking for sources, or interview subjects, there are services online that can help you. For example, I am listed with ExpertClick.com, AKA The Yearbook of Experts. Journalists can access this site to find expert sources on specific topics.

Here are two other sites you might try:

- Profnet.com/PRnewswire.com
- Women's Media Center: SheSource

Or begin asking people who know something about your subject for suggestions on who you might interview. Put out feelers and, before long, you will find yourself with some useful interview sources.

Prepare for Your Interviews

Third, always write or type a list of questions before you conduct an interview. I like to set up the questions in an order that uses the same organization I think my article (or my chapter, booklet, etc.) might follow. Later, if I choose to transcribe the tape of the interview, I can edit the transcript, writing my article as I do so. This makes the writing go much faster.

Record Your Interviews

Fourth, always tape or record your interviews and type or write notes while you conduct them. In many states, you are required by law to tell someone you interview over the phone that you are, indeed, recording them. So, be sure you are aware of the laws in your state, or simply make it a practice to tell all your interview subjects you are recording before you begin. I also type notes, even when I interview someone in person. (I bring along my laptop.) This gives me a partial transcript, which I go back and later complete using the recording. and ensures that I get as many quotes down on paper as possible, and that I do so as accurately as possible. I write quickly, but my handwriting is sloppy, and even under the best of circumstances I often can't read what I've written.

Today there are many ways to record an interview. You can use a free teleconference line, such as freeconferencecallhd.com or Zoom.com. The latter includes a transcription service, but you can choose from a variety of free and paid transcription services for other audio recordings.

Beware of "Off the Record"

Fifth, if an expert source tells you something "off the record," that means you can't use the information they just told you. It really is off the record(ing) . . . unless they say it's off the record after they tell you something. Then, you don't have to honor their request to keep the information private. That said, I always honor a request to keep information off the record no matter when the person says those specific words. I want my expert sources to trust me and allow me to come back to them, should I need them for another interview. If needed, I could always go to another source and try to get them to give me the same information *on the record.*

Sixth, don't change quotes. However, I often ask people if they'd like me to correct their grammar. No one likes to sound stupid, and my articles sound better when expert sources use correct grammar. Most people prefer to have their quotes "cleaned up."

Keep Quotes in Context

Seventh, don't quote someone out of context. That's asking for trouble.

Keep Quotes Accurate

Eighth, don't misquote anyone. Ever.

Handle the Basics Early

Ninth, at the beginning of an interview, always get the basics handled:

get the correct spelling of the person's name, their title, their address, etc. Doing this early is a great ice breaker. Plus, this ensures you don't forget to do so at the end of the interview, when you or the subject might be pressed for time.

Be Conversational

Tenth, treat the interview like a conversation. Take some time at the beginning to explain why you are interviewing the person or to remind the expert of why you are writing the article or what your book is about. Ask your source what the weather is like where they live. Do whatever you can to make the person feel comfortable and to relieve your own nerves.

Don't Agree to a Review

Eleventh, avoid agreeing to have your sources read what you've written, although they often ask to do so. You don't want interview subjects to change their minds about what they've said once they read their words.

If you must agree, let them read only their quotes and not the whole article, chapter, book, etc. If they want to read the whole piece to understand the context within which you used their quote, make sure they understand that they have no say over your manuscript. They cannot edit or change it. Nor can they edit or change their quotes (unless it's for the better).

Thank Your Sources

Twelfth, remember to send your sources a thank you note and a copy of the finished article—a copy of the publication or a link to the piece.

The best interviews I've conducted end with my interview sources *thanking me for interviewing them.* Yes, that happens occasionally. Sometimes they find the subject interesting and enjoy the opportunity to think about it and discuss it with me. On these occasions, when I hang up the phone or walk out of their offices, I feel grateful for the people who agreed to let me interview them, gave me their time, and were willing to share their thoughts and expertise with me.

I'm also profoundly grateful for the fact that my job as a nonfiction writer offers me the opportunity to interview such knowledgeable people on such fascinating subjects.

AP Style Cheat Sheet

By Nina Amir

If you are going to write for publications, you must first become familiar with style rules. I don't mean your written voice or the guidelines of the publication, although those are important, too. I mean Associated Press (AP) usage style.

While book editors tend to use the <u>Chicago Manual of Style</u>, journalists use the <u>AP Stylebook</u>, and never the twain shall meet. In fact, editors of one faction or the other tend to have strong feelings about certain idiosyncrasies of these styles. So, if you're not familiar with AP, pay close attention to this chapter.

Note that AP style differs significantly from MLA or other style guides typically used in English classes, which is why you don't want an English teacher editing your articles.

In short, the rules associated with AP style focus on accuracy, clarity, and conciseness. Knowing these rules helps you, especially if you are a new journalist seeking assignments, make a good first impression. Write your query letter in AP style to impress the editor with your knowledge of their requirements. Then, of course, do the same with your actual assignment. When you turn in a well-written and well-researched article on deadline that uses AP style, you'll quickly become one of their favorite freelance writers.

Here are 13 of the most commonly used AP rules when writing articles, essays, op eds, and other types of pieces for publication. Keep in mind that there are exceptions to every rule (and rules can change over time), so purchase a copy of the stylebook and check it often.

1. **Use a person's full name and title upon first mention in an article.** For example, write: Jason Andrews, chief operating officer of This is My Company. Once you have fully identified someone, refer to that person by last name only.

2. **Spell out abbreviations or acronyms on first reference.** For example, use National Nonfiction Writing Month the first time you refer to the event in a story. Use NaNonFiWriMo on any references made after that. Usually, the abbreviation or acronym is placed in parens right after the first reference, like this: National Nonfiction Writing Month (NaNonFiWriMo).

3. **Abbreviate months when used with days, and use numerals when referring to dates:** For instance, use 1, 2, 3, etc., not ordinal numbers, such as 1st, 2nd, 3rd, etc. Exceptions are March, April, May, June, and July; they are written out in full because they are short. Right: Oct. 2, 2015. Wrong: October 2nd, 2015. *Bonus Tip:* If you use only the month and year, spell out the month, such as October 2015.

4. **Spell out numbers zero through nine and use numerals for 10 and higher.** For example, The publisher chose to work with 10 new authors; only five of those authors had work accepted for publication. *Bonus Tips:* Numbers used at the beginning of a sentence are spelled out. Years are rarely spelled out. Use numerals for ages younger than 10.

5. **Spell out the word "percent" but use numerals for the associated number.** For instance, Participation in the NaNonFiWriMo event has increased 15 percent every year.

6. **Capitalize formal titles used before a name but never after.** Wrong: Jason Andrews, Chief Operating Officer of This is My Company. Right: Chief Operating Officer of This is My Company Jason Andrews. You can shorten or even summarize long titles, but don't capitalize that title. *Bonus Tip:* Lowercase general titles before names such as singer Bruce Springsteen or actor Robert Redford.

7. **Do not use courtesy titles.** For example, *Mr.*, *Miss*, *Mrs.*, or *Ms.* have no place in an article—except in direct quotes or where needed to distinguish between people of the same name.

8. **Use a single space after a period.** No need to say more.

9. **Do not use commas before a conjunction in a simple series**. For example: *In writing class, they learned that exclamation points, periods and semicolons are punctuation. Or this: Her sisters are Sarah, Hannah, Rachel and Leah.*

10. **Use a comma before the terminal conjunction in a complex series if part of that series also contains a conjunction**. Here's an example from owl.english.purdue.edu (a superb source for anything related to grammar and sentence structure as well as style): *Purdue University's English Department offers doctoral majors in Literature, Second Language Studies, English Language and Linguistics, and Rhetoric and Composition. To simplify the AP style rules on commas, think about it this way:* In a simple series, AP doesn't use a comma before the last item. For a series of complex terms, it does use commas after each (for clarity).

11. **Commas and periods go within quotation marks.** Right: *"I did nothing wrong," he said. She said, "Let's go to the Purdue game."* Wrong: *"I did nothing wrong", he said. She said, "Let's go to the Purdue game".* This rule applies whenever you use quotation marks. Semicolons tend to be an exception to the rule.

12. **Use quotation marks around the titles of books, songs, television shows, computer games, poems, lectures, speeches and works of art**. Right: *Author James Scott Bell published a new novel, "Romeo's Rules." They sang "The Star-Spangled Banner" before the game.* Wrong: *Author James Scott Bell published a new novel, Romeo's Rules. They sang The Star-Spangled Banner before the game.*

13. **Do not use quotations around the names of magazines, newspapers, the Bible, or books that are catalogues of reference materials.** Right: *The Washington Post first reported the story. He reads the Bible every morning.* Do not underline or italicize these names either.

If you have questions about AP style rules, check the AP site at www. apstylebook.com/. Use the rules in your writing, and you won't have to count on luck to get your first assignment.

From Pixels to Pay:
Six Tips for Writing Articles— and Getting Paid for Them

By Kelly James-Enger

There's plenty of advice out there when it comes to writing, but what if you want to do more than write? What if you want to write—*and* get paid for it? Then you must consider more than simply writing well—you have to be able to find and analyze markets, pitch ideas, research articles, and deliver what your editor seeks or contracted you to produce. If you're serious about making money as a freelancer, keep these six strategies in mind:

Go Where the Money Is

It sounds obvious, but I'm always amazed at how many new writers fail to pursue markets that pay. Yes, there are many markets that offer "exposure," but there are many more that pay for freelance material. And a quick review of them reveals the difference—websites that pay their writers are almost always of higher quality than those that fail to pay for articles.

Both print and online markets typically have their writers' guidelines listed online (most print mags have an online component). Check the guidelines to see what the market offers. If it doesn't mention pay, it's safe to assume it doesn't.

Take the Next Step

You're already getting paid for your work? Great! But as you gain experience, consider targeting higher-paying markets if you're not doing so already. As you amass clips and experience, you're better positioned to go after more competitive markets, so make that your new goal.

Re-Slant Whenever You Can

One of the mistakes I made as a new freelancer was to write one story at a time. I would come up with an idea, find a relevant market for it, sell the idea, research and write the story, and then move on to a completely new idea. I don't do that any longer. Now I try to re-spin, or re-slant, every idea I have. So, for example, I wrote a piece for a national health magazine about easy ways to de-stress. Then I pitched and wrote a story for a parenting magazine about how to help your kids de-stress. Then I pitched and wrote a piece for an online market on how exercise is a powerful de-stressor. Yes, each story is different but the basic information about the subject is the same, which means I spend less time getting up to speed the way I would with a subject that's brand-new to me.

Get the idea? Always look beyond the one story-one sale mindset. When you come up with an idea, consider different angles and different approaches you can take, and which markets would be a good fit for them, and then pitch accordingly. This technique works for older stories, too—you may come across new research that makes the topic timely again or gives you a new way to approach the subject.

Focus on Developing "Regulars"

As I said, one of my earliest mistakes was that I failed to re-slant ideas. One thing I did very well, however, is the advice I give to both new and experienced writers: focus on developing regular clients. There are several reasons for this. First of all, when you're already a known entity to a client, you're much more likely to have your pitches read—and assigned. Second, your editor is likely to think of you and assign stories that you don't even have to pitch! (About half of my work is this kind of assignment—when an editor reaches out to me with a story idea as opposed to me pitching her with it.)

When you get your first assignment from an editor, do a great job (obviously), and then pitch her with another idea. Make it your goal to turn her from a one-time client into a regular one. And even if you haven't written for a market for a while, touch base every few months to say "hi" and remind her that you're around. Even a quick base touch may result in an assignment!

Know Your Hourly Rate

When you write for print and online publications, you're typically paid per word (or, in the case of blogs, per post). That number tells you how much you'll make for completing the assignment, but it doesn't tell you what you're making per word. You may be surprised to learn that I write for markets that don't pay that much per word; some markets pay as little as $0.25 or $0.30 per word. However, I know how long the stories will take, and that I can make close to $100 per hour writing them.

Here's an example: I write for a regional parenting magazine that pays me $350 for a story of 1,400 words. At first glance, it's only $0.25 per word, and since most of my markets pay $0.50-1.50 per word (or more), you might think I'd turn it down. However, I know that the stories only require a few quick interviews to research and write; they typically take me four to five hours to complete. Do the math—that's a rate of $70 to $87.50 per hour, an excellent hourly figure.

Don't Be Afraid to Ask for More

Finally, I tell writers to be brave. Ask for money, at least once in a while. (Trust me: editors never offer raises to freelancers without being asked.) If you've written three or four stories for a market, ask if the editor can boost your rate. If a market that's new to you offers you a rate that's below your norm, don't be afraid to counter with a higher figure. Back up your request with a reason—will the story take a lot of legwork? Does the editor need a tight turnaround?

Give the editor a reason to say "yes" to your request, and you'll make more money for the story you're working on—and for more stories for that client in the future, too. And that winds up to be more money in your pocket—and your bank account.

Developing and Pitching Your Idea

By Nina Amir

*T*his chapter has been adapted from a Nonfiction Writers' University *(NFWU) assignment. Learn more about the NFWU at* nonfictionwritersuniversity.com

When you decide to write an article for a publication, you must do three things:

1. Identify publications that cover the subject matter about which you want to write—*your market.*

2. Target the publication's readership—*write for the ideal reader.*

3. Write an effective query letter—*pitch in the correct format.*

No matter the reason you want to write articles for publication or the type of articles you want to write, these steps remain imperative. If you don't target your content to magazines that actually publish articles on your topic and if you don't write articles of interest to or that benefit the publication's readers, no matter how well you pitch, you won't sell your work.

How to Develop an Article Idea

Ideas for articles come from many places. Maybe you:

- have life or work experience, and you'd like to write about that.

- know interesting people you want to interview.

- know interesting places you'd like to profile.

- like to report on news or events in your town or industry.

- like to write about your passions or hobbies.

You can write the article and then find an appropriate market—publication—for your article. Or you can find the market first, and then write the article with that publication in mind. It can prove easier to sell articles if you do the latter.

How to Research Your Markets

Your idea has to target a market both in terms of ideal reader and type of publication. It might fit a broad publication market, like women's fashion magazines. You then need to research all the magazines in that market to find the ones best suited for your article. By this I mean those that are most likely to run the type of article you want to write.

Your piece also could have a narrow market, such as people and publications interested in East Coast travel. You then need to find regional and national magazines that target readers interested in East Coast travel.

In either case, understand the readers of these publications to ensure your article meets their needs and interests. Your piece must provide them with value.

Also take into consideration who advertises in the magazine. If you can target an article in such a way that the publication can sell advertising around your piece, you may increase your chances of landing a contract.

How to Angle Your Article

Here are two tips for targeting magazines or angling your article to a particular publication:

1. Look at articles written over the last three years. In many cases, you will see a pattern. However, the angle of the articles will

change. Discover what subjects are covered yearly or every two to three years, and then take that topic, or a similar one, and angle it in a new and interesting manner.

2. Look at the types of advertisers who pay for ads in the magazines. Most magazines love it when they can bring in large advertising accounts for an article. If you can cater your piece to the type of advertisers who support the magazine, you stand a better chance of landing an assignment.

How to Write a Query Letter

Now you are ready to pitch your article. For that you need to send a query letter to someone at the magazine.

The word "query" means "a question" or "an inquiry." A query letter asks an editor or an agent if they might be interested in purchasing your work or representing you.

Research each publication to discover the name of an editor and how that editor prefers to be pitched. You usually can find the information on the publications' website.

Most editors today prefer emailed query letters. These should be short and pithy and show that you know something about the publication's readers and what they want to read.

Here's another school of thought: Longer queries answer questions in editors' minds and offer them more information, which makes it easier for them to decide. Use your judgment; don't go overboard. Respect the editor's time.

Your query should illustrate that you know something about the magazine's readers and advertisers. After all, these two groups keep a magazine in business. That said, a terrific idea backed up by your expertise will more often than not get you the job if presented well in a flawless query letter.

While emailed queries can be a bit less formal than traditional snail-mailed queries, don't make the mistake of tossing out the old query letter format. Consider your query a business letter, and include all the traditional query elements:

- an intriguing lead paragraph

- a pitch that includes the title of your article, what it is about, and the benefits it will provide to readers

- a paragraph explaining exactly how you plan to approach the subject, including word count and information on sources you plan to interview

- a final paragraph detailing why you are qualified to write the story

Never:

- call the editor

- send in a query with typos or other errors

- place the wrong editor's name on the letter

- indicate you may not have the experience to write the article

- tell the editor you would like to be published in their magazine because "you've always wanted to write"

- pitch more than one article at time

- call your own idea or work "marvelous" or "awesome"

- overdo exclamation marks, question marks or the use of sentence fragments

Your targeted idea reinforced by expertise and knowledge of the magazine will likely get you the assignment if you present a perfect query letter. Add a tie in to the publication's advertising focus, and you'll have a sure-fire sale.

Find the Right Publication for Your Article

By Nina Amir

Some writers begin with an article idea and then find a market, or publication, that seems like a good fit for the idea. Others begin with a market, first choosing a publication and then developing an idea specifically for that magazine's readership. No matter which method fits your personality or way of working, you must learn how to research markets for your article ideas.

Identifying the best markets for your work allows you to take a targeted approach to pitching publications. This strategy also increases the odds of landing more paying gigs—selling more articles—than a scattered querying strategy.

How to Analyze Article Markets

Every publication has its own market. In other words, *Time, Women's Day, Sports Illustrated,* and *National Geographic* all have distinct audiences they target. To understand their markets, you must know the demographics and interests of their readers.

Use Google to help you find magazines or newspapers best suited for your article idea. You also can go to the library's periodical section to examine different publications or visit a store in your area that sells a large variety of publications.

Additionally, a publication's website holds many keys to its target market. A good place to find such details is on the page meant to inform potential advertisers about the publication. This page often includes demographics on readers as well as details on their interests. The type of advertisers a publication wants to attract indicates readers' interests and demographics as well.

What to Analyze When Choosing Publications to Pitch

Before you pitch, analyze a few key things about a publication's market. Start with readers' age range, location, and interests. Also, determine if the publication has themed or seasonal issues, like an Easter, health, or money issue, and how often the magazine is published.

Analyze the advertisements as well. If the publication runs ads for local businesses only, you can confirm its local focus or the regional range. If it features ads for high-end, expensive jewelry, cars, and clothing, it's safe to assume its readers are in a high-income bracket. Studying advertisers is a great way to come up with article ideas as well.

Also, analyze the publication's previously published articles. For instance, if you want to write about health programs for men over 50, read articles published on this or adjacent topics in the last three to five years. Propose a new take on the subject—one they haven't covered in that period. You can even explore articles dating back 10 years, and pitch articles on topics covered a decade ago; you can rest assured the topic is aligned for the magazine and its readers (unless its focus or demographics have changed) and its time for an updated piece. Study the publication's recurring columns and the types and length of feature articles it runs. Where would your piece fit? For instance, is it appropriate for a featured article, a column or even the "shorts" section at the front of the publication? Knowing this helps you pitch more accurately.

Don't forget to examine the bylines. Some magazines only publish articles by experts. Others require contributors to pay for publication rather than getting paid. (Notice if an article written by someone is followed by an ad for their company or service.) And some publications use their in-house staff to write everything, which means there is no room for freelance contributors. They also may have ongoing contributors, such as a writer who produces a monthly column. Review the masthead to find names of editors; compare these names to article bylines. If they match, the publication uses in-house writers. But always check the publication's writers' guidelines to determine if the magazine or newspaper accepts freelance contributions.

Choose Publications to Pitch

With this research completed, you are ready to finalize your list of publications to pitch. Choose 10 markets that seem like a good fit for your article. Then prioritize them. You can query simultaneously, if the publications all allow that, or individually. The latter requires that you wait for a response to your query before submitting to the next publication on your list, which makes pitching a long process.

Or decide on 10 markets that fit your expertise and interests; then use the information you gathered to brainstorm articles ideas you can pitch to one or more of them. Again, you can pitch simultaneously or individually, depending on the publication's guidelines.

Once you have even one publication chosen, you are ready to send a query letter to the correct editor pitching your article idea. Use the market information you have gleaned to show the editor you understand their publication and can write for their readers.

How to Write a Query Letter for Magazines and Other Publications

By Nina Amir

*T*his chapter is adapted from a Nonfiction Writers' University (NFWU) challenge. (Learn more about the NFWU at <u>nonfictionwritersuniversity. com</u>.)

Let's delve a bit deeper into the correct practices for producing an effective query letter. If you want to write articles with the intention of becoming a freelance writer, promoting your book, or writing for publication occasionally, you need to know how to do this. Whether you're trying to land your first assignment and byline or your hundredth, learn how to pitch publications using a query letter.

Your pitch puts the ball in the mitt. In this case, the mitt symbolizes an editor's hands. If the ball, which symbolizes your query, drops out of the mitt, you've lost the editor's interest, and you'll likely get a rejection note thrown back and end up on the bench. If the ball stays in the mitt, and then get's thrown to one of the bases (goes to an editorial board meeting), you could make it back to home base and score a run—land an assignment.

Yet, there's more to a query letter than the actual pitch. The whole letter sells the article idea. Much like a book proposal, a query letter for a publication of any type serves as a marketing document. It's also a business tool used to show a publication editor that you:

- have a good idea

- can write

- know the audience

- have angled the article idea for that market

- have the appropriate expertise and experience

- can complete the job

When you put all the parts of a query together, you create a successful pitch. You sell the piece to a publication.

The Five Publication Query Letter Sections

To write a query letter for a publication, first, develop your article idea. Be sure to research your market, find the best publication or publications to pitch, and angle your idea appropriately.

Then include these five sections in your query letter:

1. Pitch paragraph or lead

This must be your most compelling paragraph. It's the actual pitch. You want the editor to catch the ball you throw and hang on to it. You don't want it thrown back. You want to get a home run.

Consider using the lead to your article here; this often works well. Here's an example of the first paragraph of a query to *Dance Spirit Magazine* that landed me an assignment. It also became the lead to the article:

> *What happens when you combine the music of Charles Parker, one of the most influential musicians in jazz history, with the Emmy Award-winning choreography of tap dancer Jason Samuels Smith and the skill of three of the most talented female tappers in the world today? You get the most extraordinarily unique and intricate footwork put to the sounds of classic bee bop and executed by women who can get down, be bad, kick butt, and attack the choreography just like all the great male*

hoofers that preceded them—but who can do it with a feminine and sexy vibe to boot.

2. Article description and detail

The second paragraph of your query letter should include the title of your article and all the details about how you will complete the assignment. Include the number of words you plan to submit, keeping in mind the magazine's requirements. Here is the second paragraph of my query for the Dance Spirit Magazine article:

I'd like to write an article for Dance Spirit Magazine on Jason Samuels Smith's newest production, "Charlie's Angels: A Tribute to Charlie Parker." This 1,500-word article, called "The 'Bad' Women of Tap," would focus on the phenomenal level of accomplishment female tappers have reached in the dance world today, the old stereotypes about female tappers they are breaking, and the experience three women — Chloe Arnold, Dormeshia Sumbry-Edwards and Michelle Dorrance — have had to date performing in "Charlie's Angels." This new, female-only tap show set to Parker's music and choreographed by Samuels Smith currently includes just five numbers, and all three women perform solos. For all the performers, the experience of mastering such difficult choreography and performing it together has been a unique experience unlike performing in an all-women's tap company, especially since the choreography and the music were both created by men. In addition, the level of dance required of the women makes their performance historic. This article would include information gleaned from interviews with Arnold, Sumbry-Edwards, and Dorrance, as well as from Samuels Smith. If you prefer, as a sidebar to the story I could provide an interview with Samuels Smith focusing on how he came up with the idea for "Charlie's Angels," how he chose the first three women to perform the work, his plans for lengthening it into a full-length production, why he wanted to showcase women tappers, and his mission not only to show the relationship between dance and music but to show people "what music looks like" as well.

3. Bio and credentials

Provide a brief bio including your pertinent credentials, experience, links to work you've had published, etc. If you have any other information that might help land the writing gig, include it as well. Here's my third paragraph for the same article query. (Please note that some of this information is now outdated including the website address; the article was published years ago.):

> *I am a journalist, author and editor with 28+ years of experience working for more than 40 different national, regional, and international magazines, newsletters and newspapers on both a freelance and full-time basis. If you would like to review my résumé or peruse some of my clips, please visit my website at www.copywrightcommunications.com. The fact that I have been intricately involved in my son's dance career for the last 10 years and am a lover of dance in general has given me a good working knowledge of this art form. Plus, I already have a relationship with both Arnold and Samuels Smith. Thus, the combination of my writing experience, knowledge of dance, and connections in the tap world makes me uniquely suited to write this story for Dance Spirit Magazine. Also, if you recall, I contacted you previously. Some time ago, Jeni Tu from Dance Teacher magazine, a publication I have written for in the past, suggested we speak in conjunction with a book I'm writing about mentoring boys who want to become professional dancers.*

4. Conclusion and contact details

End on a positive note. I usually write a few sentences in a final paragraph saying I hope to hear from the editor and providing my contact information. Here's the final paragraph to my *Dance Spirit Magazine* query:

Thank you for considering this query. I hope you agree that a story on these three amazing female tap dancers and the unique show in which they currently are performing would make interesting reading for your audience. I look forward to hearing from you. You can reach me at [email address] or at [phone number].

5. Salutation

Keep it simply. "Sincerely" works well.

Remember to proofread and edit your query. You don't want to have any mistakes. A typo—especially in the editor's name or first paragraph—will result in a rejection.

When you put all the parts of a query together, you get a complete or successful pitch. But don't forget the following two steps.

Angle for the Market

To write a query letter for a publication, you need to complete the following six steps.

1. **Research your market.** Find the best publication or publications to pitch. Take time to study different magazines or publications that cover the topic about which you want to write or who cover topics of interest to the readers you want to reach. Become familiar with those magazines, their readers, their advertisers, and their content. If possible, read 12 months of back issues. In the process, locate the name of the correct and current editor to whom you should address your query. If you are unsure of which editor to select, check the magazine and its website. If the magazine has departments, find the editor responsible for that department. If you can't find the correct editor, try an associate editor, who is more likely to give it some time and attention than a top editor. If all else fails, try one of the top editors (usually not

the managing editor); they will have assistants to direct your query to the right person. Spell that person's name correctly; Choose formality over informality (Ms. Amir vs. Nina). Find out the preferred method of communication (email or snail mail). Do not call.

2. **Angle your idea.** Craft your article idea for that publication and its readers. I don't recommend writing an article or essay first and then looking for a market; it's harder to sell pieces that way.

Follow these seven steps to increase your chances of producing queries that sell. After all, pitching is not simply about the ball you throw landing in an editor's mitt. Your words need to make that editor want to hang onto the ball.

How to Develop a Compelling Query Lead

By Nina Amir

The first paragraph makes or breaks your article or query. Without a strong "lead," no one reads past that point. If they only read the first paragraph, you won't sell your article to a magazine, let alone influence its readers.

You must write the lead to your query with these four points in mind:

1. The lead of your query (the first paragraph) must entice the editor to buy the article—to offer you a contract.

2. The lead launches your query—starts it—but can be identical to your article's lead.

3. The lead provides an ending point; your article's final paragraph should tie into the lead.

4. Your lead should arouse justifiable curiosity and foretell something of what lies ahead in the rest of the article.

The Chicken and Egg Problem

Writing a lead to an article or query prior to composing the rest of the piece can feel difficult. It's a bit like the old chicken-and-egg problem. You might wonder, "How can I write a good lead to an article when I don't yet know how I will organize the pieces of my story or even what content I will include?"

On the other hand, without a lead, you might wonder, "How can I organize the pieces of my story when I have no clear notion of how it is to begin?" In fact, the lead to your article sets the stage for the whole piece. Everything about your article flows out of the first paragraph.

The Four Primary Types of Leads

It's easier to write a lead when you have a few types from which to choose. Here are three often-used leads.

1. Startling Assertion Lead

This is a straightforward and dramatic lead that confronts the reader with an unexpected fact or statement. It is followed with a general statement. This is a great option if you want to get into a story quickly. It's not effective for more complex stories, and it lacks the human touch you need for a personality profile. Here's an example:

Early in 2014, five women at [breast care center] had their breasts removed in solidarity with the women diagnosed with breast cancer. These cases dramatize the extremely emotional and complicated issues involved in surviving and avoiding this deadly disease.

Here are two more subtle versions, quoted from *How to Write a Magazine Article* by Jake Hubbard:

The economy, declared one of the president's top advisors, is going to get worse before it gets better.

It is not who you know but what you know that counts in the field of nuclear engineering.

2. Round-Up, Bam-Bam-Bam or Bullet Lead

If you need a way to enter into a story that involves material scattered across time or geography, this lead does the trick every time. It works well for trend stories.

To write this type of lead, highlight a spread of changes using bullets or italicized sentences, and then link them to a general statement. Use no more than four, no less than two bullets in the lead.

For example:

- *Facebook now charges to boost content on the site, which is the only way to really get page content seen in a target market.*

- *LinkedIn has added a site-specific blog feature to help users get their content noticed by their ideal readers.*

- *And Pinterest now offers users the opportunity to run ads targeted at potential customers.*

While social networks began as a place to meet old friends and connect with business associates and potential clients, these moves indicate a clear change in focus from "social" to "business" networking on these sites. In fact, many social networking sites are struggling to find ways to make money, and their new strategies mean business users have more options—but they have to pay for them.

3. **Indirect Lead**

If you want to arouse curiosity in your readers quickly, approach the point of the article in a roundabout way. Begin your article by telling a story, describing a place, or relating some sort of history. Then loop into the main theme of the piece with a general statement.

Here are six types of indirect leads:

- **Anecdotal**—begin by telling a story.

- **Scene setter plus general statement**—begin by describing a scene, then add a statement that provides context or explanation.

- **Recap plus general statement**—recapitulates a historical situation then introduces a new twist.

- **Question**—start with a query to the reader.

- **Quotations and Dialogue**—use a quotation or dialogue between two people as your starting point.

- **Compare and Contrast**—use the differences between two things as entry into your article.

Additionally, you can use witty definitions, commands, surprising twists, and shocking statements as indirect leads.

4. **Newspaper lead**

Not only is a newspaper lead effective for newspaper articles, it can be used for query letters as well (as can all the other leads).

To write a newspaper lead, include "The Five Ws and an H":

- Who
- What
- Where
- When
- Why
- How

Additionally, employ the "Inverted Pyramid" when writing a newspaper lead (or a newspaper article structure). In other words, lead with your strongest material. Do not use the first paragraph to warm up. Instead, shoot first with the best material you have. Answer questions and offer minor details later.

With this arsenal of lead options, you should never find yourself struggling to begin your query letter. These leads work well for articles, too.

HOW TO WRITE DIFFERENT TYPES OF ARTICLES

How to Write
Magazine Articles and Essays

By Nina Amir

D^o you dream of writing for a living, but you aren't sure how? Or have you considered writing a full-length book, but that feel too difficult? If so, it's time to consider writing newspaper or magazine articles. Put your pen to paper or your fingers to keyboard, and whip out an essay or a reported piece of writing.

I love being a journalist. I get to write about so many interesting topics and people and things that interest me. For example, once I was asked by *Movmnt* magazine to write an article on the Cirque du Soleil show, *Believe*, which was opening in Las Vegas. I had a blast learning all about its creator, Criss Angel, and writing about the people who helped him bring his dream into reality. I also wrote an essay for InterfaithFamily. com on something personal—my struggle with my husband's loss of faith. I wrote a reported article for the same "ezine" on how to prepare for the Jewish holidays of Rosh Hashanah and Yom Kippur. Before that, I wrote a reported article on the state of the organic market for a trade journal called *Grocery Headquarters,* a piece on teen suicide for *Bay Area Parent,* and a story about how dancers maintain healthy feet for *Dance Spirit* magazine.

If you've never written a magazine article or essay, don't be put off. It's not that difficult. Just tell 'em what you're gonna tell 'em, tell 'em, then tell 'em what you told 'em. At least that's what the late Professor John Keats used to tell us. (It sounds just like what most students are told about how to write an essay.)

Let's break down the main parts of an article.

The Three Parts of an Article

1. ***Just tell 'em what you're gonna tell 'em.*** An article consists, first, of a lead, or a first paragraph, that entices the reader into your article. This could also be comprised of several paragraphs if you choose to use an anecdote, a few bulleted items or discussion of a trend. After that, however, you need a sentence or a few sentences that tell your reader what the article is about—a statement of purpose, if you will. Tell them what the article is about so they have an idea of where they are going if they continue reading. Hopefully, you've enticed them into wanting to go there.

2. ***Tell 'em.*** This section represents the meat of your article. Place all your supporting material here, such as statistics, quotes obtained from interviews, additional anecdotes, analysis, etc. Remember, however, that if you write for a newspaper, in most cases you must compose your piece in an un-slanted manner, which means without an opinion. If you write an essay, you may voice your opinion as loudly as you'd like. Also, if you write an essay, rely on your own "voice" and experience or expertise not quoted sources. Most magazine articles are slanted to the author's perspective, and this remains true even in reported articles.

3. ***Tell 'em what you told 'em.*** Now write your conclusion. Sum up what you wrote about without simply repeating what you already said. That's right: Say it again but in a totally new way so your readers have no idea that they are reading the same information again. Give the topic a new angle. Put a new take on it. Offer additional information to support what you've offered previously. For an essay, if possible, provide a broader view or some quote, anecdote, or bit of information that takes the reader into the future. You can use this tactic with a reported article as well, but it works especially well with essays.

If you are looking for a topic to write about, ask yourself what interests you. Prof. Keats, like most good teachers, always said, "Write about what you know." I tend to look at my life and identify issues with which I'm currently struggling. I query magazines and newspapers with those topics, and I typically find the editors receptive. Most people are just like you. They face the same challenges.

I have a caveat to the "write what you know" advice: Know about what you write. A good writer/journalist can write about anything at all by becoming the expert on that topic. I've written about life insurance tax law, immortality, retail store imaging, Kabbalah, geodesic domes, lobbying, and supermarket pet aisles. I served as the managing editor and primary writer for two international medical newsletters, *Same-Day Surgery* and *Clinical Laser Surgery*. For the most part, I didn't know much at all about these topics when I began writing about them. I knew a lot about them afterward.

The biggest compliment I ever received came from an employee at the Equitable Life Assurance Society of America. I worked there for a year and a half as the associate editor of employee communications. I had just written and published a long and detailed article in the employee newspaper about life insurance tax law. She came up to me and said, "That's the first article on the subject that I've ever understood." I told her, "I had to understand it to be able to write about it."

So, pick a topic for an article or essay, preferably one you are interested in or feel passionate about. Learn everything you can about the subject. Understand it. Then write about it using the basic article structure outlined here.

The How-To Article:
10 Things You Should Know

By Zachary Petit

As anyone with an Internet connection and a problem knows, there's a *lot* of bad advice out there.

Think back to the last time you wanted to know how to fix your kitchen sink. Or replace your toilet tank. Or do something more outside the box, like, say, safely dye your dog's fur green so he can be Yoda for Halloween.

You typed your quandary into Google in search of a solid how-to—and up came 10,000 unreliable websites that specialize in how-tos but offer less-than-stellar advice. This deluge of (poorly written!) and often downright inaccurate info may get a lot of us journalists seeing red (not to mention whatever poor dachshund is about to be turned green), but there's one good thing to come of all this: *It means great how-tos are more valuable than ever.*

How-tos, or *service pieces*, as they're often called, are simple and fast to write, and everyone from newspapers to magazines to websites publishes them—which makes them an excellent gateway to breaking into a publication. In other words, they're an ideal type of article to test-drive.

So, let's do our civic duties as journalists and save the kitchen sinks and dachshunds of the world.

Here's how to write a good how-to.

1. Choose Your Adventure.

First, you've got to pick a good topic. Brainstorm away. This is one of the easiest parts of the process: Just start with your expertise. What do you know in a way that nobody else does? Flex that knowledge. Then brainstorm more and consider what problems you've recently solved—did you just lose 25 pounds for your wedding in a short timeframe? Quit smoking? Build a creative desk? Ideas abound. Tap into your own curiosity, and chances are you'll tap into someone else's. Another good way to generate salable ideas is to browse publications and see what rises from the ether for each magazine listing. And/or, try taking a big story—say, a swine flu outbreak story you saw on CNN—and turn it into a small piece: how to tell if you've got swine flu, regular flu, bird flu, a cold, hypochondria, etc.

2. Do Your Homework.

What's it going to take to pull this piece off, and to pull it off the right way? Make a list. Try banging out a rough draft.

Ask yourself: Do you have enough knowledge to pull it off on your own? Even if you think you do, go deeper: What links and resources can you provide readers who are looking for supplemental info? Would the piece be enriched by quotes from experts or statistics you've dug up? Even if you know exactly what you're talking about, people like to see a chorus of consensus.

3. Know Your Reader.

Set a goal of who you're going to be writing to: the expert. The layperson. The dabbler. The desperate Googler. All of them at once. Cater your material to that specific type of person, and after you're done, consider actually *showing* it to someone you know who fits that description. Does it all make sense to them, and get them where they need to go?

4. Be Deep.

There's nothing worse than finding a how-to on exactly the topic you're seeking, and then realizing that all of the info is bare-bones, overly obvious basics totaling 75 words. So, anticipate all questions your reader may have, and answer them. Be like narrative nonfiction author Richard Ben Cramer, who said, "I'm out there to clean the plate. Once they've read what I've written on a subject, I want them to think, 'That's it!' I think the highest aspiration people in our trade can have is that once they've written a story, nobody will ever try it again." Sure, writing Pulitzer-grade prose on conflicts in the Mid-East is slightly different than writing a 500-word story on how to keep squirrels off your birdfeeder, but the same principle applies to all good journalism.

5. Be Deep . . . But Be Careful.

Like a diver, the deeper you go, the more pressure there is on you. You've got to get everything in your how-to right. Don't trust the Internet. Trust your own experience with your subject; trust experts; fact check everything; field test everything. Getting it right builds trust with editors, who will be giving you future assignments, and moreover it builds trust with readers, who will be embarking upon the very experiment you're proposing.

6. Don't Be Afraid of Your Own Voice.

Obviously, the info is king in a how-to, but don't hesitate to let a little voice shine through (*if* it's the type of thing your target market will be okay with). Voice is what will make your prose uniquely yours. So be yourself. Readers will probably be able to tell if you're trying to be anything else. Some people will like it, and some people won't. (It took me a long time to be comfortable mentioning dachshunds dressed as Yoda in articles.) As Jack Kerouac, himself no stranger to voice, said, "It ain't whatcha write, it's the way atcha write it." (Still, never forget that with a how-to, it's easy for a voice to get too loud too fast.)

7. Be Chronological.

This step probably should have come a few paragraphs ago in this article. But still. It'll make your piece exponentially easier for a reader to follow.

8. Be Succinct.

Hunter S. Thompson: "Not a wasted word. This has been a main point to my literary thinking all my life."

Tom Clancy: "I do not over-intellectualize the production process. I try to keep it simple: Tell the damned story."

9. Polish to Perfection.

As in all writing, this is vital, but especially here. If you're writing a piece about how to view the meteor shower that's happening next weekend, and you make an obvious gaffe like misspelling *meteor* or getting the name of a constellation wrong, how can the editor believe you'll be able to pull everything else off correctly, from the names of experts to accurate quotes to the best viewing locations around town?

10. Seal the Deal.

Finally, make sure you *finish* the piece and actually submit it. Cast your fears aside, and put your work in someone's hands, trusting they might want to know *exactly* what you've just written.

Sure, you should overanalyze your piece, but you shouldn't overanalyze it so much that it never leaves your desktop. After all, as Philip Roth said, "The road to hell is paved with works-in-progress."

And hell is a long way away from that meteor shower everyone is wanting to see.

How to Write a Q & A Article for a Magazine

By Nina Amir

A few years ago I wrote an article for a social media magazine based upon an interview I conducted with bestselling author T. Harv Eker. When the magazine asked me to do this interview and article, I jumped at the chance despite my busy schedule. Why? One of the best parts of my job as a journalist involves getting to talk to interesting people, especially people I admire or whom I consider great teachers. Eker falls into both categories. Also, the magazine just needed a Q & A article, the easiest and fastest type of article to write.

I heard Eker speak about 10 years ago at an event. He addressed the audience for two enthralling hours. I'd been trying to make it to one of his intensives ever since. When I received the assignment to interview him, it seemed like a gift from heaven, except for the fact that I was supposed to interview the author of *The Millionaire Mindset* about social media rather than the topic of his book or courses. I'm interested in social media, too–and how to succeed at it. So, the assignment still felt like a gift.

I began my preparations for the interview by crafting a set of questions. Eker's PR person had sent me a list of his standard interview questions (based on his book), but they weren't suited to the magazine's audience or focus. So, I rewrote them and added a few additional ones. I sent this revised list to Eker's PR person for approval.

However, Eker refused the rewrite of his standard list of questions. When my questions were rejected, I revised again and went back with a version close to his original questions. That meant I would speak to him primarily about his area of expertise and squeeze in just one or two questions related to social media, the focus of the magazine for which I was writing.

Whoo hoo! Fun for me, and I'd make it work for the magazine by angling the information toward their readership.

How to Prepare Your Interview Questions

Most people you interview will not have a set list of questions. They'll allow you to ask questions you create specifically to fulfill the needs of the magazine for which you are writing. These should be pertinent to the expertise of the person you interview and to your article topic.

Writing a Q & A article is one of the easier types of magazine articles to write, and you can employ the same technique on your blog quite successfully as well. In fact, interviews with well-known people posted on your blog drive traffic to your site. Magazines love these articles for the same reason; a celebrity of any type drives magazine sales, subscriptions or online views.

I like to start my questions with one or two that allow me to delve into the person's background. Sometimes the information garnered here ends up in the introduction. I may rewrite their bio using some unique information I obtain from these first questions. Plus, it breaks the ice for the more serious questions to follow.

Next, I create a set of questions that flow logically one after the other and allow the interviewee to make the points I am seeking. In this way, the article flows logically from one question and answer into another. I won't have to move any of the answers around.

Producing the Manuscript

Now comes the difficult part–at least if the interviewee was a willing participant eager to speak about his or her topic. You have to edit and cut the transcript of the interview to a manageable word count. For example, after my interview with Eker was transcribed, I ended up with an 8,600-word document. My article assignment called for a 2,000-word piece, including an introductory paragraph or two. That meant a lot of cutting of superb information.

You have to go through the transcript and cut and slash. If that isn't possible, you need to read carefully and cut sentences and or phrases, then combine what is left with ellipses (. . .) to show you have removed some of what the source said.

Of course, you also must edit the parts of the transcript you choose to include. You cannot change your subject's words, but you can delete redundancies and add appropriate punctuation, etc. At the time of the interview, I always ask the person's permission to correct their grammar as well.

You need a lead, or introductory paragraph or two, as well as some sort of description of the person (a bio)–either included in the lead or placed at the end of the article, and sometimes a conclusion.

Pretty simple, really. No need to craft a lot of content. The interview subject provides that. And you go away having met someone interesting, learned something and acquired one more byline and paycheck.

With this particular Q & A piece, I ended up with a refresher course for the time I heard Eker speak. I received a mini, one-on-one Millionaire Mind Intensive. I was pretty happy about that. Plus, the interview was published as a cover story. Not bad all the way around.

How to Turn Current Life Issues into Writing Topics

By Nina Amir

The best topics for personal essays, researched articles, blog posts, information products, and even books can be found in the current life issues with which you struggle. Sometimes you may not directly experience these challenges; you may see your family members or friends dealing with them. However, if you want answers or solutions to their problems (or your own), you've found fodder for a publishable piece.

More than likely, someone besides you or the people you know faces the same challenge and seeks a similar answer or solution. They want a prescription for their pain or a way to transform their life. That means a market exists for your piece.

Identify Your Challenges

How do you turn your current life issues into writing topics? First, ask yourself:

- "What am I struggling with right now in my own life?"

- "What problems are those I love struggling with that I'd like to find solutions to?"

Use your answers to create topics for articles, essays, or blog posts. These may become a springboard for a book.

Seek the Answers and Solutions You Need

Now comes the fun part. Interview experts to get the answers, solutions, or advice you seek. Then share what you learned with readers who struggle with the same issues. In other words, write an article based on your findings.

Of course, if you have found solutions through your own life experience, share what you have learned in your article. This approach makes you a subject expert.

You also can combine first-person accounts with expert research. I enjoy this option the most. It allows you to put a personal touch on the article, essay, or post, but also backs up your experience and knowledge with that of other experts. Plus, it produces a written piece jam-packed with great solutions readers want and need.

I've done this on numerous occasions with situations involving my children. For example, when my children ended up attending four different elementary schools, I became worried about how that might affect them. I proposed a story on the topic to a regional parenting magazine. They published "The Ins and Outs of Changing Schools," which also landed me their publishing company's Best Practices Award for a local feature.

When both my children were involved in competitive sports-related activities, I wondered how that stress would affect them. I proposed a story to the same magazine. They published "The Competition Dilemma."

I moved into national magazines with a story about dancers' foot problems after my son, a dancer, incurred several foot injuries, and I wanted to know how he could prevent them in the future. (I mentioned this assignment previously.) *Dance Teacher Magazine* published "Fancy Footwork."

A number of years later I wrote a piece for the same regional parenting magazine based on my family's experience with teen suicide. (I also mentioned this assignment previously.) I queried them because I felt that even their audience, which consists of parents with young children, should be made aware of the prevalent problem in the community and how to prevent and deal with it. The essay was based solely on my own thoughts, but I did interview an expert and offer advice in a sidebar, and it accompanied a story on bullying. It was called simply "Teenage Suicide."

LI & Business published a story of mine based on my experiences as an author coach. I discussed how writers can use social networks to help write their books. I didn't interview anyone; I was the expert source. I've written a number of articles on boys in dance "off the top of my head" and numerous essays on Jewish and spiritual topics this way. For instance, "I wrote If God Were Sitting at Your Sabbath Table, Would You Notice?" and published it at JewishMagazine.com.

All of these articles and essays create platform for books I want to write. And that's something important to think about. The topics that interest you because they are issues or problems with which you grapple make great book ideas. The same is true of areas you know something about that other people know less about—or that may hold interest for others. Why? Because most readers of nonfiction books purchase them to solve problems, learn how to do something, find out how to handle issues they are having, or somehow create change in their lives. That's also why they read magazines.

Create an Idea File Based on Your Life

Your life issues may be the best article idea file you can find. In other words, look to your life for article and essay ideas. If you are struggling with issues, the likelihood is that others are as well. That means an editor somewhere will be interested in your idea.

Don't worry about the fact that you don't have the solution to the problem when you propose the piece. You can interview experts who do (and list those experts in your query).

Today, make a list of:

1. the problems you wish someone would solve for you

2. the issues you face

3. the challenges in your life

4. the things you know

5. the things you wish you knew

6. the things you are good at

7. the things you wish you were good at

Now write a query letter based on each one of these topics. Next, research the magazines that might be interested in your proposed article or essay. Then, send out those queries.

You may not think you are an expert in anything, but you are. Everyone knows something about something. You have had experiences. You have gained knowledge. Maybe you know how to keep the deer away from your plants or how to grow really great lettuce. Maybe you know how to teach children to love learning languages or to paint. Maybe you know the best places to hike in your neighborhood or how to care for a diabetic cat. Some publication wants that knowledge—and so do their readers. That means they will buy your work.

10 Ways to Use Life Story in Nonfiction Writing

By Nina Amir

An intersection exists between memoir and other types of nonfiction. Indeed, there are many ways to use your life story besides producing a memoir.

These include the following:

1. You can use your life story as anecdotes or vignettes for a lead into a researched article. You can do so as the conclusion to an article as well. Plus, anecdotes offer superb ways to illustrate the points you make in an article.

2. Your life experience can provide the premise for a researched article; then you can use anecdotes to illustrate your points or simply as a lead into the piece.

3. You can expand on #1 or #2 and write an entire researched nonfiction book based on your experience.

4. You can use your life story as the premise for a personal essay.

5. You can create a blog on a topic related to your memoir and write posts and publish them.

6. You can take the lessons you learned during the events detailed in your memoir and write about them in more detail; offer how-to articles, advice columns, coaching columns, interviews with experts, etc.

7. You can choose to write about a hobby or some other area of interest in which you have some experience (or in which you are willing to get experience), and then include your experiences in the book.

8. Create information products that solve problems and include information about yourself and how you came to find the solutions.

9. Create information products based on your life experiences— ones that would have helped you—and include your experiences (good and bad) in the product.

10. Compose how-to-write-better articles using anecdotes about your writing process.

If you like writing memoir or using your life stories or experiences in your writing, these 10 ideas should keep you busy for a while!

Using Personal Experience in How-To Articles

By Nina Amir

Often writers want to use life stories and personal experiences in their writing, but they think the only way to do so involves writing a memoir. That couldn't be further from the truth. In the last chapter, I offered 10 ways to use life story in nonfiction writing. Now, I'd like to expand on how to do so in an article.

Most articles are written by an expert or by a journalist or writer who has interviewed experts and then compiled and analyzed the information obtained into a cohesive format. The articles that lend themselves to life story, personal experience, and anecdote are how-to, features, and personal essay. In this chapter, we're going to focus on how-to articles.

When you learn something from your life experience, you become an expert and can write an article that offers people advice, steps, or some other form of prescriptive information based on that expertise. You also can take your experience and expertise and back it up with the authority of other experts. This entails interviewing them and then including the information they provide in your article. Quoting them in your article lends credibility to your work and your own advice.

How to Structure Your Life-Experience How-To Article

An effective structure for a how-to article that draws on personal experience might use an anecdote or vignette as the lead, or first paragraph, of the article. This entices readers into the article by creating a scene or describing the issue you plan to discuss. Follow this with a line or two, possibly even a paragraph, that describes the actual point of the article. Basically, tell the reader what the piece is about or what value or the information you will provide.

Next, in the body of the article, lay out all your data, steps, resources, quotes, and other helpful advice. You might even weave in some anecdotes about how the steps worked for you or how different pieces of advice helped you along the way. If you have interviewed experts, maybe they have anecdotes you can add in into the body of the article.

Finally, end with another anecdote or vignette, if possible. If you don't have one, conclude with a summary of the advice you offered.

Every day you add to your body of experiences, or you encounter new issues, problems, and challenges. All of these provide ample fodder for articles in which you can use your life story.

Using Personal Experience in Essays

By Nina Amir

For the memoirist or anyone who enjoys sharing their life experiences, it makes total sense to write personal essays. This form lends itself well to anecdote and vignette.

Essays tend to be short pieces written from an author's personal point of view. While many types of essays exist, the personal essay offers those who like to write about personal experience a chance to describe and expound upon these things. They also can analyze their experiences and offer information from their own lives that might prove useful to others in a much more artistic manner than allowed by an article. However, unlike memoirs, essays don't always read like fiction, although they can contain dialogue.

The Personal Essay Format

Consider writing personal essays using a three-part or four-part format. Begin with an anecdote or vignette. Set the stage. Describe a scene. Depict an issue with which you are struggling. Tell a story.

Next, explain why that experience or story was important to you. How did it impact you? Are you still struggling with that particular experience? What did you learn? How did you deal with it? How did it change you?

Now, discuss why the experience might be important for your reader. How does your life story and experience relate to them? What can they glean from it? How can they put your lessons to use in their lives? What benefit does your story have for readers?

Last, in the final paragraph or two take the subject broader. Relate it to something more than just you or your reader. Find a universal lesson or principle to discuss. End in a manner that gives your story appeal to more people or makes it relevant to anyone anywhere. Drive this point home.

If you can't find a way to make your essay universal, end with another story that drives your point or theme home.

Pretty simple, really.

Last, look for magazines that publish personal essays or Google some of your favorite magazines that publish personal essays and find out how to submit yours.

Other Essay Formats

Many other essay formats exist. Do some research, and decide which one suits your writing style or topic best.

- Narrative essays tell a story, often focusing on a specific event or experience.

- Descriptive essays focus on creating a vivid picture for the reader through detailed language and sensory details.

- Reflective essays explore the author's thoughts and feelings about a specific experience or topic.

- Argumentative/Persuasive (Op-Ed) essays present a viewpoint on a topic and attempt to persuade the reader to agree with the author's position.

- Expository essays explain a topic or concept, often from a personal perspective.

- Braided essays weave together multiple threads of narrative or reflection, creating a complex and layered story.

- Fragmented essays are composed of smaller, unconnected pieces that create a mosaic-like effect.

- Visual essays use images, photos, or other visual elements to complement the text.

- Lyric essays employ poetic language and techniques to explore personal experiences.

- Flash essays are short, impactful essays that capture a moment or idea in a concise way.

- Hermit (Horseshoe) Crab essays take on existing forms (like social media posts, instructions, etc.) to structure the essay, basically pretending to be something they are not

- Collage essays are written experimental form contemplating a subject using fragments of narrative and found material.

- Descriptive (portrait or profile) essays often take the shape of: "Let me tell you about this difficult and complex person I used to know. I learned a lot from him, I realize now."

It's a good idea to find out a magazine's submission guidelines prior to beginning to write your personal essay. That way you'll know how many words they require or what special needs they have before you start writing. You also want to discover if they want a query prior to essay submission or a query with submission attached. Then, you can cater your article to their specifications, which gives you a better chance of getting your personal essay published.

Writing from your personal experience can be enormously rewarding. Since your life changes all the time, you never run out of essay or article ideas. Plus, the numerous and creative ways to compose essays ensures you can use your life to illustrate a point and never get bored doing so.

How to Write a Personality Profile

By Nina Amir

There's a reason magazines like *People* are so popular. We love to read about celebrities and interesting personalities. If you enjoy these types of articles, of if you enjoy interviewing people—and would jump at the chance to meet and get to know your favorite actor, author, or local politician, for example—learn how to write a personality profile.

I learned how to write a personality profile at Syracuse University from Professor Jake Hubbard, who had written for *National Geographic* and authored a book called *Magazine Editing for Professionals*. I'll always remember how I almost flunked my first attempt to write a profile of singer Willie Nelson. The assignment was based not on an interview but on a jumble of facts and quotes given to us. Despite my bad grade, I learned how to write a personality profile and went on to write many of them. In fact, the *Greenwich* (CT) *Times* had me write a series of personality profiles of celebrities living in its community.

The following is Professor Hubbard's "formula," or structure, for a successful personality profile. Follow it to the "T," and you'll produce a winning personality profile every time.

1. **Lead:** Create a lead that paints a picture of the person you are profiling. A natural affiliation exists between the anecdote and the personal profile lead. Find an anecdote that accurately portrays your subject's character, and craft a lead out of this story.

2. **General Statement:** Follow your lead with a sentence that explains why the anecdote describes the personality of the person. In other words, sum up the essence of the person.

3. **Justification:** Tell people why this person is one they should be interested in. Offer diverse achievements that are not deducible. For example, he owns 15 Rolls Royces (he's rich), has 14 mistresses (he's charming or a playboy), and writes a magazine column read by two million people (he's smart, well-known, and talented). Also, raise a question based upon the diversity that coexists in the person. This is your best shot at catching the reader's attention.

4. **Amplification:** Offer a description of or details about what the person is doing. These might be achievements that are not as diverse but are recent in the person's life.

5. **Wart 1:** Cast the individual in an unfavorable light by providing a negative characteristic. You can accomplish this by asking the person about their faults or weaknesses. Interviews with their friends and family can provide this information as well.

6. **Flashback:** Include anecdotes from the past and history, including past achievements, until you catch up to the present.

7. **Wart 2:** Shed light on another negative characteristic. These make your subject more believable. No one is perfect.

8. **Whither:** Discuss what the person is going to do next. Discuss their future projects or what is in store for them.

9. **Get Out of Town:** Finish off your profile piece with a final anecdote. This should weave back to the essential characteristics of the person and evoke resonance with the lead.

Final Tips on Writing a Personality Profile

The easiest way to produce a personality profile is to create a list of interview questions based upon the structure above. After your interview, make a conclusion about your subject. Then write.

Also, look for signposts—information you can use to warn the reader of a new phase in the story. Follow these with data. For example, if you are writing about a personality that is accused of a crime, you could say, "The case against So-and-So looks strong. The attorney has several pieces of evidence, including . . ."

Consider using a final quote at the end of the piece (or near the end) to stress your own opinion about the person. As a journalist, you can't say what you think. You have to remain objective, but you can slant your piece to "show" your opinion.

Finally, be sure to use transitional phrases between the structural sections of your personality profile, such as at beginning of the Amplification, Flashback, and Whither sections.

Although it can feel difficult to follow this structure, I promise editors will love the end results. And after you've written one or two, you'll understand why this structure works so well for personality profiles.

8 More Types of Magazine Articles

By Nina Amir

In this section, you've learned how to write eight types of articles. However, there are other article formats you might want to try, including the eight listed below.

1. **Trend:** As the name implies, a trend article showcases an increasing or decreasing movement over time, such as in housing prices, the number of people voting, or couples getting divorced.

2. **Lifestyle:** These articles focus on a lifestyle issue, such as health, relationships, or recreation, and can include interviews as well as statistics. Such a piece might discuss the private school options in a city, how to use a new walking path in a town, or the best restaurants around town.

3. **Shorts:** Many publications feature short pieces, typically at the front of the magazine. These might be 150-500 words in length. Topics vary but always focus on the target market of the publication. Sometimes a magazine has a section on health and fitness, for example, and it might consist of four to five short pieces on the topic.

4. **Book Reviews:** This type of article is self-explanatory—read a book and discuss the pros and cons of the subject, story, and writing. Reviews are opinion pieces, so feel free to speak openly about your perspective.

5. **Movie Reviews:** Like a book review, this article involves watching a movie and then writing about the pros and cons of the story, acting, lighting, costumes, scenery, music, and cinematography. Again, this is an opinion pieces, so don't be afraid to share your point of view.

6. **Restaurant Reviews:** Like a book or movie review, this article format involves visiting a restaurant, eating several dishes, and providing your opinion on the food, service, and restaurant in general. It is also an opinion piece.

7. **Op-Eds:** These are the most common opinion pieces and are found in most newspapers. Pick a topic about which you feel strongly—could be about politics, crime in your town, or the increased cost of housing—and share your perspective on the issue. You can even include proposed solutions to the problem you address in the piece.

8. **Evergreen Articles:** Such articles are the staple of most magazines and stand the test of time, rarely becoming outdated. They tend to be about topics of continued interest to an audience; however, it is your job to cover that topic with a new and unique angle. For example, most general interest magazines run pieces related to holidays, like Valentine's Day, Easter, or Christmas. Health and fitness publications cover weight loss or exercise routines on a regular basis. Financial publications cover taxes in March and April. These all represent evergreen topics.

You are now armed with a total of 16 different magazine article formats. Develop an idea for each format, write a query letter for each idea, and you may find yourself with 16 assignments.

HOW TO LAND YOUR FIRST ASSIGNMENT

5 Ways to Get a Magazine Article Published

By Nina Amir

Both magazines and book publishers purchase manuscripts for the same reason: to make money. Magazines make money with ad sales, subscriptions, and newsstand or in-store purchases. Of course, many magazines now are available online as well and make money via subscriptions or online advertising. Book publishers make money purely through digital and print books sales.

What does this mean to you, the aspiring journalist or author? If you want publishers to purchase your manuscripts, you must find a way to help them make money.

With that in mind, here are five ways to get a magazine article (or book) published:

1. **Help sell ads**. When it comes to magazines, newspapers, and online publications featuring advertisements, the way to help them make money involves creating an idea that sells ads. I used to write for a trade publication, and the articles they assigned me always catered to their advertisers. Look at any major magazine; you will see ads focused on the audience of the magazine and the types of articles running in that particular issue. Advertisers help keep publications in business. Find the publication's editorial schedule and propose an article the ad reps can sell around, and you'll surely sell an article as well. You also can research keywords that pull in people that might

purchase related items. How-to articles that lend themselves to related salable items work as well.

2. **Add value.** Provide a solution to a problem. Articles (and books) that fill a need in the marketplace and in readers lives tend to sell well. They make good business sense. If you can show that many people will find your manuscript useful, publishers will see dollar signs and purchase it.

3. **Prove a large market exists for your manuscript or idea.** If many readers want or need the information you plan to provide, publishers will start counting the dollars they will make from your article (or book). Lots of readers equates to lots of sales. That means you have helped the publisher make money.

4. **Reach a big audience by having a platform**. A "platform" is a built-in audience or readership for your work. If you can prove that lots of people know who you are and love to read what you write or what you have to say and will, therefore, run out and buy a copy of your book or the magazine that has published your article, publishers will purchase your writing. A big platform coupled with a good idea represents a sure-fire way to get your work published—even if you aren't a great writer.

5. **Be a good businessperson.** Be more than a writer. Be a promoter and marketer, too. When a publisher of any type realizes that you can help promote your article or book, your odds of getting a contract increase tremendously. Publishers want good business partners, not just good writers. Good writers don't always make publishers a lot of money. Good businesspeople who happen to be good writers make publishers a lot of money. If you are both—or are willing to work at being both—you increase your odds of selling your work to a publisher.

Land Your First Assignment with a Niche Magazine

By Nina Amir

Niche publications remain super resources for writers who want to build freelance businesses or expert status. If you have no bylines to your name, a publication targeted to a specific audience, such as crafters, writers, Christian business owners, people living in Silicon Valley, or motorcycle enthusiasts, can provide you with your first. Niche publications tend to be open to new writers with expertise in the magazine's subject area.

You may have heard about the decline in the newspaper and magazine markets in recent years. Yet, remaining successful publications often aim for relatively niche groups and realize they have to fight to retain and gain readership. If you have an expertise to provide to a niche audience, a magazine editor might find your queries welcome. You can hang out your shingle as an expert quite easily by writing for a variety of publications in one niche.

Even though Americans spend less time reading magazines compared to other media, magazine publishers are surviving, improving their products, and even coming out with new publications. In 2024, the global digital newspaper and magazine market was valued at $36.18 billion and is expected to grow to $47.05 billion by 2030. Many magazines have become "luxury items" according to Bloomberg, and long-form journalism, high-end photography, and publications like *Vanity Fair, Vogue, The New Yorker, Architectural Digest* continuing seeing a steady audience of readers. On the other end of the spectrum, niche publications have seen a resurgence and are finding success with their readers in print as well.

You are a Subject Expert

Over the years, I've enjoyed writing for a variety of niche publications that cater to my interests and areas of experience, such as regional parenting magazines, dance magazines, and spiritual newspapers. Such publications tend to be welcoming to new writers, especially if you are a subject expert. Thus, pitching a niche publication might be a perfect initial step to becoming a journalist and getting a first byline.

Don't overthink your expert status. You are an expert on something—including your life. I wrote for parenting magazines because I was a parent; I pitched articles related to issues my children or I faced and interviewed experts for solutions to those problems.

Consider what you know and are interested in. Then, find publications that cater to others who share that interest. For instance, if your friends constantly ask you for advice about gardening, you are a gardening expert. You know more than someone else about gardening, and a gardening publication will appreciate your wisdom and perspective.

Four Steps to Writing for a Niche Magazine

To write an article for a niche magazine that caters to a subject in which you have expertise or that helps you establish topic-related expert status, follow these four steps:

1. Research publications that cater to audiences interested in your area of expertise. Make a list of the publications for which you'd like to write.

2. Choose an article subject unique to one or more of the publications you identified or that has a unique angle on an evergreen topic that will interest the publication's audience. Make sure the idea is targeted to the magazine's audience.

3. Choose the type of article you will write. Study the magazine to determine what kinds of articles the editors typically publish. It's possibly they have a "shorts" section at the front of the magazine; this can be a good place to break in. Or you can propose a longer article. (The next section of this book provides a variety of formats from which to choose.)

4. Query the publication. Do this before you write the piece, or at least before you submit the finished article. Most publications do not like unsolicited manuscripts, and some don't accept them.

5. Submit your article on time once you get an affirmative response to your query.

Writing for a niche publication differs little to writing for any other magazine or newspaper. The only difference is that its content remains subject specific in each issue, and niche magazines want and need articles written by subject experts. If you are a subject expert, pitch a relevant idea to a niche publication and you are highly likely to land your first assignment.

Land Your First Assignment with a Regional Publication

By Nina Amir

Many nonfiction writers have aspirations of writing for newspapers or magazines. Plus, many authors of nonfiction books find it necessary at times to write journalistic pieces to establish themselves as experts in their field or to publicize their books. To develop a career as a freelance journalist, though, you first have to land a writing assignment. Then you have to complete that assignment so well that the editor wants you to write for the publication again.

Begin Your Career Writing for Regional Publications

A great place to begin developing this type of writer/editor relationship is with a regional publication. I have a soft spot in my heart for regional publications. Not only did I get my first "clips" or by-lines writing for regional newspapers and magazines while I was still in high school and college, upon college graduation I went to work as a writer and editor for a regional magazine. I continued to work full-time for regional publications for a few years before moving on to other jobs in publishing, but I've never stopped writing for regional publications. In fact, regional publications have remained the mainstay of my freelance writing work everywhere I've lived.

For the beginning journalist, regional publications provide a wonderful way to begin accumulating the clips you need to prove to national publications you can write and produce professionally crafted and researched articles. For the seasoned journalist, they provide numerous article markets and a continuous source of revenue.

While living in California, I often wrote for *Bay Area Parent* magazine's Silicon Valley Edition. My editor there welcomed my queries and came to me with ideas she knew fell within my realm of interest. I also wrote articles several times for a Silicon Valley magazine; a few years after the last piece was published, the editor reached out with an article idea. "I immediately thought of you when I was deciding who should write the piece," she said.

How to Pitch a Regional Magazine

Here are five things to keep in mind if you decide to pitch a regional publication:

1. **Think dollars.** To pitch a regional magazine, keep in mind some of the tips offered in the chapter on *5 Ways to Get a Magazine Article or a Book Published.* Propose a piece that makes the publication money.

2. **Know the magazines territory.** Don't pitch articles outside the area covered by the magazine. Create an idea that involves an organization or event within the market area.

3. **Know the readership.** You will endear yourself to the editor if you show you are up on local politics, regional issues, school problems, and business trends that impact the publication's readers. Know the market and what concerns the magazine's readers.

4. **Know the magazine.** That brings us to an obvious tip: You must have read the magazine and know what types of articles the editors prefer. Cater your article ideas to what the magazine tends to run. Look at old issues for ideas. Don't pitch ideas they covered previously.

5. **Become a psychic.** Develop the skill of seeing into the future. You have to have a big picture view . . . be able to look into

a crystal ball and predict what the regional magazine's readers will be interested in several months from now.

Regional magazines don't tend to pay a lot, but they can be a great source of revenue if you develop a relationship with several of them. Write for them on a regular basis, and this becomes the foundation of your writing business and a great way to land early clips.

How to Score a Magazine Assignment...
And Get Asked to Write a Second

By Jill Wolfson

As the editor of a monthly regional parenting magazine, I get some jaw-dropping queries from people who want to write for us. I think I can speak for most editors when I say: Here are some ways NOT to approach an editor. I've taken these verbatim from my inbox:

Hey Jill,
I'm a real journalist, so I could probably whip out something for your rag real fast.

Dear Editor,
I have no writing experience, but I think my child is really funny and I could write about that.

Dear Editor,
I want to write for you. Give me some ideas and I'll do them.

And my all-time favorite:

Dear Editor,
I have no journalism experience and I'm not a parent, but I'm a real brat magnet. My nephew likes to jump on the bed when he comes to visit.

Now that you know how *not* to approach a magazine editor, here's some advice on what will get her or his attention—and, importantly, what will keep that attention for future assignments. Just because a publication is regional or a give-away doesn't mean that it doesn't adhere to high journalistic standards.

1. **Before you approach an editor, know the publication.** Study at least six back issues. Nothing turns off an editor more than a query on a topic that recently ran or a topic that clearly isn't right for the magazine. Almost weekly, I get an email from someone who tells me how much *Bay Area Parent* needs a humor column from a mom's point of view. Hello! We've been running the same mom humor column for six years.

2. **Contact the editor and ask for the Writer's Guidelines.** Take them to heart. If the guidelines say that most stories are written in a light tone and are between 500-1,500 words, don't think you are going to sell a 10,000-word investigative article. Try another magazine for that one.

   Follow procedures for submitting. If the editor asks for a query, send that before submitting a full article.

   Be patient about getting a response. If you haven't heard anything in two weeks, it's okay to send a polite follow-up. Remember, be persistent but not obnoxious.

3. **Come up with your own ideas, and present one or two at a time.** My head starts spinning if I get a list of 15 story ideas from a writer with whom I never worked. It also tells me that the writer isn't particularly passionate about any of the ideas.

4. **Do your research before you present the query.** Be very clear about the idea. You should be able to give the gist of the story in one or two clear paragraphs. If you can't, it's probably a sign that you aren't clear about the idea in your own mind. I also like to get a brief list of people who will be interviewed for the article.

5. **Take special note of departments in the magazine, and tailor your pitch to one of them.** When I'm working with a new

writer, I frequently like to assign a shorter story (such as a Q & A or news brief) before letting a writer tackle a full-fledged article requiring multiple sources and a complex structure. You'll find it easier to break into a magazine if you take this approach.

Hurray! You got an assignment. Now you need to know how to develop a successful editor-writer relationship. Here are a few tips and issues to keep in mind:

1. **Let the editor know if the story is taking a different shape as soon as possible.** Things change during reporting; an editor understands that. If major shifts occur—a change in the agreed-upon angle or a major source who will no longer be quoted—alert the editor immediately. No one likes a big surprise at deadline.

2. **Make the editor's job easy, and you are likely to become one of the go-to writers.** Turn in copy on time or even before deadline. If possible, ask someone to proof your article for spelling and grammatical errors. I don't mind a few errors, but I get really concerned about a writer when an article comes in full of typos and bad grammar. What does that say about his/her fact-checking?

3. **Be amenable to making changes in your story**. That doesn't mean being a push-over, but be flexible when working with the editor to make your story the best it can be. Typically, the editor knows his or her particular publication's audience and might need a story "tweaked" to emphasize certain angles. If asked, make the extra call for additional research or rewrite the lead. Try to do so with enthusiasm (or at least pretend enthusiasm).

4. **If you have certain extra skills, flaunt them.** Can you provide quality photos with your articles? Great! Can you interview parents in Chinese? Wonderful! Do you have skills specific to the magazine or the article? For example, are you an expert

knitter writing an article about crafting with children? Be sure to mention this.

Regional publications frequently use less-experienced writers than national publications do. We may pay less, but writing for regional publications provides a great way to break into nonfiction writing. By writing for this market, in a short time you can build an impressive portfolio of clips.

How to Effectively Blast Out Queries

By Linda Formichelli

Your plan is to write articles for magazines, but you don't want to spend time writing without an assignment. You also realize it can take a some time to land an assignment or have enough of them to keep you busy . . . and provide steady income. So, blast your way to success with a month-long query challenge: Write four queries and send your completed pitches off to at least one magazine per day for 30 days.

Here's how:

1. *Make time.* Guess what? You don't find time, you make it. If you're waiting for time to magically appear in your busy day where you can do nothing but interview, research, and write, the next four weeks (or for months) are going to come and go without a single pitch leaving your email account.

   Schedule time for writing into your calendar daily, because if you don't make this time a priority, I guarantee something else will come along to fill that slot.

   You may have to get up early, stay up late, or say no to some obligations—or even to some fun stuff. But don't worry—it's just for 30 days, so keep your eyes on your goal of succeeding as a freelance writer.

2. *Batch your tasks.* Avoid feeling scattered and work faster by batching similar tasks. For example, generate all of your ideas at once, then research markets for all of them. Schedule your

interviews at one time, and try to group them together so you can bang them out.

3. **Don't over-research.** Too many writers get bogged down in piles of notes and hours of interview replays. Do only as much research as you need to do to write your query.

For the query process, limit interviews to two or three, and keep them to 10 minutes each. Do just enough research to help you formulate intelligent questions for your interviewees and to gather stats for your pitch.

The thing many over-researchers forget is that if it ends up you don't have enough info, you can always go back for more. So, take a chance, stop researching, and start writing.

4. **Transcribe as you talk.** Transcribing interviews can be one of the most time-consuming aspects of writing query letters. If you can type fast, try transcribing the interviews as you do them, using abbreviations and made-up shorthand where necessary. Then, you won't have to go back and read an entire transcript, which is time consuming.

If you're not much of a typist (I'm not), it may be worth it to hire a transcriptionist for this challenge or use an AI transcription service. This might mean learning new technology, but it's worth it to get those pitches out there!

5. **Write fast.** If you're the kind of writer who agonizes over every word, the query challenge will overwhelm you. Try this: Read your notes, read your interview transcripts, and write your query all in one draft. If you can't think of a word, want to add a quote, or need to add in a bit of research, type in "TK" (a placeholder used in journalism circles) and move on. You can go back and fill in the TKs later.

The trick is to just get that first draft done as quickly as you can without getting bogged down in making difficult decisions on word choice and so on. You'll be surprised at how much you can get done this way.

Then, put the draft aside for a few hours and come back to it with fresh eyes—and your red pen.

6. ***Beat the fear.*** For new writers, getting one query out is scary. Getting out one a day for a whole month can be terrifying!

Remember, the writers who succeed aren't necessarily the ones with the greatest talent for prose. Even the most talented writers fail if they keep their writing locked up on their computers. The ones who succeed are the ones who send out their writing despite the fear—and keep doing it, learning from their rejections and developing a thick skin.

How to Get Your Personal Essay Published

By Writer's Relief

Writing a personal essay is a personal experience—and as such, what matters most is your experience of your writing and your satisfaction with the work you've done. But if you'd like to see your personal essay published in a literary journal or magazine, here are a few specific things you can do to help ensure your work will get a strong read:

1. ***Keep it short.*** Thanks to the Internet, the days of long, rambling personal essays and memoirs are gone. Most modern readers are rushed, distracted, and looking for some level of instant payoff when they begin to read an essay. At Writer's Relief, we advise our clients not to write essays that are longer than 3,500 words. And if you're thinking of targeting online literary magazines (which are a great resource), you may want to aim for an even lower word count. With short prose, less is more!

2. ***Get engaged.*** No, we're not talking about weddings. We're talking about current events and the modern world. Essays that are reflections on the way we live today—especially those that tackle "big" issues in a personal way—are often favorably received at literary magazines. So, if you can put a personal spin on a big issue—like foreclosure, obesity, racism, or any other social issue—you may be able to get a foot in the door at a literary magazine.

3. ***"Tell me something I don't know."*** You've heard there are no new ideas. But the fact is, no one can replicate your particular view of the world. For that reason, editors at literary magazines continue to accept prose that offers new viewpoints of modern work and play. But in order for your prose to be compelling, you've got to push for deeper, more surprising, and more insightful explorations. You're competing for space when you submit to a literary magazine, and if your insights are stronger than the competition's, then you're in!

4. ***Check your ego at the door.*** Just because you're writing a personal essay, doesn't mean you can indulge in your every last whim of hedonism. Essays that are about "me, me, me" and "I, I, I" are not likely to be published. Strive to paint a bigger picture—to show how your experiences are relevant to all people—and you'll turn editors into fans.

5. ***Submit your essays to the best-suited editors.*** If you're going to submit your personal essay, you've got to know the right people to send your work to. At Writer's Relief, we've got a database of thousands of editors who are accepting essays—and we track which editors like what specific type of work.

But you can also do this kind of research on your own. Spend time at the library or on the Web to determine which magazines are right for you, then send out your work regularly. Expect rejections and strive for acceptances. Although the odds may seem staggering, we see writers' work being accepted all the time!

While personal essays are personal, it's helpful to know what readers and editors are looking for when they read your work. We hope these tips will help you get published. Happy writing!

HOW TO LAND YOUR SECOND ASSIGNMENT

Land a Second Magazine Assignment (with the Same Publication)

By Seth Mendelson

As publisher and editor of seven different magazines, I am approached frequently by freelance writers about writing and photo assignments. Freelance writers and photographers are important to our operation, because they offer different voices and can accomplish things that my full-time editorial staff cannot. They also can fill a void in a crunch.

Why a Magazine Hires Freelance Writers

Most importantly, freelancers can offer our magazines perspectives from various parts of the country. Based in New York City, our full-time staffs tend to have a distinctive East Coast bias, one that is not good for any national publication trying to reach out to a broad section of consumers or business officials.

That said, the freelance writer we look for must come with certain attributes. Of course, they must understand the markets we serve, who we are trying to reach and what our readers are demanding from our magazines. Offering a different angle on a story concept is much desired. Also, they need to come prepared with story ideas and concepts.

Why an Editor Hires a Writer More than Once

As could be expected, the most important aspect of using a freelance writer more than once is the simple fact that they were able to submit a well-done, completed assignment on or, hopefully, before deadline. It is also crucial that the freelancer make him or herself available for any follow-up questions and assistance.

I use about five to seven freelancers every month and, during certain periods of the year, can use as many as a dozen freelancers during a particular publication cycle. Like any editor, I have my favorites; they are the ones who offer expertise on the subject matter, hand in timely and complete stories on deadline and are willing to give 100 percent all the time.

It is not hard getting one freelance assignment from me. Reach me at the right time and in need, and I am willing to give just about anyone a shot. Getting the second assignment is when things get tough.

The five most common mistakes writers make that ensure they won't be given a second assignment are:

1. Doing a bad or sloppy job.

2. Turning in an incomplete story.

3. Missing a deadline.

4. Not following assignment guidelines.

5. 5. Being uncooperative.

As for #5, in addition to not doing what you are asked, this can mean being too attached to your words. If you are writing on assignment for a publication, remember the magazine or newspaper is your "client." You need to make them happy—even if that means cutting or changing what you have written.

A Writer's Checklist for Finished Work

By Nina Amir

How do you know when you are ready to turn in your article, essay, blog post, or marketing piece to your client? I use a "checklist" for finished work. If you can tick off all the items, you are highly likely to make your client happy and get additional assignments.

What needs to happen before your work gets sent out to an editor, agent, or publisher? As a journalist and author, I constantly think about the quality of work I send out. This does not mean just the quality of my writing. It also means whether I am sending material that has been fact checked, proofread, and formatted correctly. I have to be sure I've met word counts, gathered and sent photos, quoted people correctly, and spelled names and companies correctly as well—not to mention that I have to be sure I've made sense and gotten my point across succinctly.

If you can afford to hire an editor or proofreader before you say, "finished," that's always best. However, not everyone can do so, and even I don't always have the time or money for that for many of my assignments, projects or blogs. (These days, you can use AI editors, like Grammarly, to edit assignments.)

For this reason, over the years I've come up with a checklist of things all nonfiction writers should ask themselves before they claim their projects are finished and turn them in or send them off for consideration. The checklist doesn't provide a foolproof methodology, but it reduces about 95 percent of the errors you would have otherwise.

Nina Amir's Finished Work Checklist

1. Have I said what I meant to say?

2. Have I written as concisely as possible?

3. Have I written as simply as possible?

4. Have a used the style appropriate for this publication?

5. Does the piece fulfill the request of the client or purpose and scope outlined in the contract?

6. Is the article the correct length?

7. Are all the names spelled correctly?

8. Is the manuscript formatted correctly?

9. Is my conclusion as strong as my lead or introduction?

10. Have I read it aloud to find errors I might miss when proofreading or editing on the hardcopy or computer screen?

11. Have I let the piece sit for a few days or more and then reread it to help me edit with more perspective?

12. Did I run the spellcheck function in my word-processing program?

13. Have I used an AI or grammar program to edit and proof the piece?

14. Have I read the piece with a critical eye?

15. Have I asked someone else to read my piece?

16. Have I searched out every passive verb in my work and changed it to an active verb or changed the sentence structure to allow for an active verb and stronger sentence construction?

17. Have I tightened each sentence by cutting out unnecessary words?

    If you go through all 17 points on this checklist, you'll submit much more "finished" work than you would if you didn't bother to take the time to do so.

    Here's one final step, which I include because I've rarely found a finished work that couldn't be improved in some way—a word changed or one typo fixed.

18. Forgive yourself when you find a mistake in the work you've already turned in or published.

Errors are not the end of the world. You might still land the literary agent, get the publishing contract, receive the article assignment, be awarded the freelance job, or win the writing contest.

We all make mistakes. Most of writers still succeed, and so will you. If your work comes back due to an error, correct the mistake and send it out again.

9 Things to Do before You
Turn in an Article

By Zachary Petit

Before rocketing a tin can full of people into the clouds, pilots do something amazingly simple to reduce the daunting set of complexities before them: They tick off items on a checklist.

Sure, writing is less high stakes than safely transporting the Johnston family from Cleveland to Orlando. But if you take your craft seriously and want to excel at it—and do so in the quickest and most efficient way possible—then you need to make sure you're covering all your bases before you send any article to an editor.

As a writer, this is what I run through before I turn in a piece. As an editor, this is what's going to make me strongly question your ascent, cruising altitude, and landing while you've got me on board.

It's easy to overlook the simple things, especially when you're moving fast. So, before you turn any piece in, run through the following for the sake of your editors, fact checkers, and most importantly, your readers.

1. *Reread your original query, the assignment, the contract, and/or any correspondence you may have had with your editor.* Is everything in the piece that should be? Consider this your in-flight GPS. (And make sure you wind up at the right place.)

2. *Format your story in the publication/website's style.* (Publications follow a hierarchy when it comes to style—

generally, their house style first, and then AP Style for anything not covered in there.) When somebody writes an article for me in AP Style, it says a lot about their experience and writing savvy, and those writers inevitably tend to be the best writers. (Don't know AP Style? <u>Check it out</u>.)

3. *Make sure all your proper nouns are correct—source names, organizations, products, places, etc.* Get this wrong (and you'd be amazed at how many people do), and your editor will break out in a cold sweat and make sure they're near an exit row.

4. *Fact check your piece.* And I mean really go through it, top to bottom. Question everything. Verify everything. You don't want your editor to break down in tears because that great story that's nearly at press turns out to be ¼ true. *For Bonus Miles:* Cite links/books confirming the facts in your story in the Track Changes function of Microsoft Word. Some publications I write for require this, and while it's time-consuming, it's worth it. Not only does it make an editor's life easier and maybe win you future assignments, but it also gives you a layer of confidence that the work you're producing is truly solid.

5. *Include a source list at the end of your story.* Simple enough: Just a list of the names of everyone quoted, their titles, and their email addresses or phone numbers.

6. *Double check the quotes featured in the story.* You don't ever want anyone accusing you of misquoting them, so quickly check your recording and/or notes to make sure you're spot-on. *For Bonus Miles:* Include a transcript of the interviews you conducted. Nothing polished and print-ready, just a resource for the editor to verify quotes, understand context or pull additional material if needed for something like a Q & A. When people do this for me, it's the equivalent of the free wine you get on transatlantic flights: Delightful.

7. 7. *Read your final draft as an outsider.* By now you've

probably lost objectivity for the piece. Disconnect for an afternoon, and then go back through the article with a faux-fresh eye. Ask yourself: If you were a reader, what questions would you be asking? What's missing in the narrative? What doesn't make sense or requires further explanation? These are the questions your editor will be asking—and they may require time-consuming edits if you don't tackle them now. Some writers I know read their work aloud because they feel it helps them come at it fresh. Don't hesitate to call in a trusted eye, either.

8. ***Make sure that if you were asked to provide art or photos, they're attached and properly credited.*** Trust me, you don't want to overlook that credit, as it could give both you and the magazine a black eye when you're trying to make a good impression.

9. ***Include an updated bio.*** An editor will likely be asking for it, anyway, so get the jump on them and pop it in there up front.

In my humble, non-expert opinion, the essence of being a good pilot is doing your job well enough that your passengers aren't staring up at the ceiling, wondering if the oxygen masks are about to deploy. Go through this checklist so your editor isn't scrambling around the cabin in search of a parachute.

All systems go?

Go.

10 Ways to Become a Sought-After Magazine Journalist

By Nina Amir

When I received an email from a regional magazine asking if I'd be willing to write a cover article for the publication, I happily agreed. Not only would I get paid a reasonable fee, the article would help me build platform in a subject area of interest to me.

How did this editor find me? I've written for the magazine several times before—and once on the same subject. However, the primary reason the editor of this regional parenting magazine sought me out specifically to write a story was simple. She knew I was an expert in the subject area.

The piece answered the following question: Why does dance benefit children? I've become an authority on dance and children. In particular, I'm an expert on boys and dance. Not only have I written about boys and dance for national magazines, but I also have a blog on this topic, called My Son Can Dance and a thriving Facebook group by the same name. (I don't post to the blog much since my son became a professional dancer more than12 years ago.)

I created the blog because I wanted one day to write a book on the topic. I figured the blog would help me build author platform, and it did. Additionally, I have written articles on the subject and about dance in general. The editor knew this and was familiar with my blog. When it came time to find a writer for her story about the benefits of dance for children, she immediately thought of me.

Become a Specialist

If you want to write for regional or national magazines, you can write about almost anything. However, you increase the likelihood of landing assignments if you specialize in one or two subject areas. This also increases your chances of editors thinking of you for particular types of stories.

These days, however, you want to make sure you are discoverable online as well as in print publications. Sometimes editors search for experts just as you might search for a product or service—by using their favorite search engine. Therefore, ensure you are "visible" online. This increases your chances of an editor calling or emailing you out of the blue with an assignment.

10 Ways to Become a Subject Expert

To get started, consider what articles or books you plan to write. Can you group them into one or two subject areas? If so, begin doing the following to help you become known as a subject expert:

1. Begin a blog or blogs related to those subject areas.

2. Write articles on these topics for online publications.

3. Develop a website that features your subject expertise.

4. Produce a podcast or radio show on your topic.

5. Produce YouTube videos on your topic.

6. Write guest posts for other bloggers who publish on the same or similar topics.

7. Query radio shows and podcasters with show ideas that relate to your subjects.

8. Write articles on these topics for regional magazines.

9. Query national magazines with articles on these topics.

10. Create online courses related to the topics.

You can become a subject expert in many ways, including by starting a blog. Writing researched articles on a subject also make you an expert over time and increases your expertise.

5 Surefire Ways to Make an Editor Hate Your Article

By Linda Formichelli

Your goal is probably to churn out as many articles as you can. I know you want to make sure none of these articles are ever published—because then you would have a bunch of money you don't know what to do with—so you're on the lookout for fatal *faux pas* you can commit that will doom your articles to obscurity.

If you want to make an editor hate your article, be sure to stick to these five common snafus.

1. Bury the Lead

Instead of jumping right to the point with a heavy-duty statistic, an emotionally compelling anecdote, or a strong quote, make an editor toss your article aside by doing a lot of throat clearing before getting into the meat of the story.

Many writers make this same mistake, which possibly stems from fear of laying it all out there. They feel the need to give a lot of background information, so readers know what they're getting into. The bad news is readers won't bother slogging through all the preamble to find out what you're really writing about.

Some writers also over-research their stories and try to cram in all that information at the top of the article so it's not wasted.

Readers not reading and editors throwing their hands up in despair? Success!

2. Go Under/Over the Word Count

To allay the risk that an editor will like your article and actually offer you filthy money for it, consider the word count of the magazine department you're targeting.

Typically, you would want to come in at or slightly above the average word count, but remember, you're trying to avoid the terrible circumstance of having a published article. So, write to whatever word count pleases you!

After all, sometimes you're on a roll and the prose you're crafting is so amazingly awesome that it would be a shame to delete any of it. The department you're targeting may run articles that are only 500 words, but if you send the editor 2,000 words, she'll be able to practice her editing skills by slicing out 1,500 of them.

And sometimes, the section you're aiming for runs 800-word articles— but you just can't seem to make it that far. You can scrape up only 400? Send them in and let the editor worry about the rest.

Ignore the word count, and your chances of getting an acceptance are blessedly low.

3. Don't Interview Anyone Except Your Own Sweet Self

Here's a foolproof way to make an editor ditch your article: Use yourself as the expert, and don't interview anyone else.

Magazines rarely run articles written by experts without any other sources—unless the writer happens to be super famous. And when they DO run such articles, they rarely pay for them as the editors figure the expert is writing the article as an ad for himself.

Even if you ARE an expert in topic X, typically you would use that expertise to help you know where to research, who to interview, and what to ask them. In other words, your expertise informs the article but isn't the main focus. Every fact you write in an article, an editor is going to expect you to back it up from a primary source such as research study or an interview with a top expert who is not you.

Don't risk having an article accepted by interviewing other people! Just write from your personal knowledge of the topic.

4. Interview Only People You Know

Maybe you don't want to totally aggravate an editor by not interviewing people, but you DO want to anger him just a bit. The solution: Interview only people you know.

For example, if you're writing a health article for a national magazine, interview your doctor and your best friend's doctor. When working on an article for a newsstand women's magazine, ask your neighbors and local friends for quotes.

How will this ensure an editor won't buy your article? Well, national magazine editors expect your interview sources to be ethnically and geographically diverse—but still within the magazine's demographic—and they also want the experts you to interview to be at the top of their field, not merely ones you happen to know.

Instead of contacting organizations, think tanks, universities, online forums, and source-finding services like ProfNet (profnet.com) and ExpertClick (expertclick.com), be sure to take the lazy route by interviewing the people on your speed dial. The editor is sure to spare you a big fat check!

5. Be Boring

Many magazines feature a conversational, easy to read, and even edgy writing style, so your job is to be as boring, stiff, and formal as possible.

For example, NEVER use contractions—instead, always say "You are," "It is," and "They have." Use five-dollar words like "utilize" and "equivocate" instead of their shorter, easier counterparts.

Rather than using strong words that invoke just the image you want to portray, rely on plenty of weak adjectives and adverbs, plus intensifiers like "very" and "really." And be sure to include lots of passive verbs and long, unwieldy noun phrases instead of punchy verbs and nouns.

Writing in a stilted, businesslike manner is one of the main ways to keep an editor from wanting your article.

Your mission: To not have an article accepted. The outcome: Accomplished!

HOW TO MONETIZE YOUR WORK

How to Earn More and Work Less by Managing Your Rights

By Michael Sedge

Thirty-nine years ago, I walked out of my last job, determined to be a writer . . . and have been fulfilling that role ever since. I've published thousands-and-thousands of articles, 30 books, written four TV documentaries, advertising copy, and children's plays. I have been a freelance editor in one form or another—i.e., contributing editor, travel editor, managing editor, senior editor, European correspondent, war correspondent, Mediterranean and Africa editor—to over 40 publications and news agencies. I have turned my writing into a number of successful spin-off businesses–Markets Abroad Newsletter, Strawberry Media stock photo agency, The Sedge Group, Michael-Bruno, LLC—serving such clients a The Associated Press, Newsweek, Time-Life, National Geographic, Mobil Oil, General Dynamics, Lockheed Martin, Discovery Channel, MCI International, Department of Defense, and Department of State.

All of this and, according to my friends, I only work half-a-way. While that may be a misconception—they do not see me at the computer in PJs at midnight or 4 a.m.—it is possible if one approaches their writing career with two key principles: (1) it is a business and (2) the world is your market.

While at the height of my writing career, I only produced 23 articles a year (while working on books, documentaries, and other activities). That is fewer than two articles per month. At the same time, however, my byline appeared approximately 207 times in global publications while my annual article income exceeded $50,000.

The secret? I was selling each article an average of nine times to publications in various countries and languages around the world. Put into mathematical terms: 23 articles a year x 9 sales per article = 207 published articles. I received an average of $250 per article x 207 = $51,750 annual income.

You, too, can make more and work less if you learn to work smart, manage the rights to your articles, and consider the world your market. The following is an excerpt from my book, *Marketing Strategies for Writers*, that will get your started.

Sometimes I feel that writers intentionally make an effort to fail as businesspeople. Take, for example, the thousands of freelancers around the world who write articles. They produce a feature, sell it, see it in print, and then begin work on another story. It too gets written, sold, and printed. Then a new article is begun. It becomes a vicious circle.

Now some would say that this is a pattern of success. I am here to tell you that it is a blueprint for excess work, below-average income, and ultimately, writer burnout. Why? First, given that the average article of one thousand words sells for approximately $375 in the United States, writers need to produce and sell eight articles a month if they want to earn an annual income of $35,000. Writing this many quality articles every thirty days is a huge task. Then, of course, because freelance writers are independently employed, they are required to spend a large percentage of their annual income on social security taxes, health insurance, and income taxes. After all these taxes and insurance payments are made, most writers—even those selling articles regularly—find themselves walking the tightrope of poverty.

If they would only approach writing as a business, however, this dire situation could probably be avoided. Let's imagine for a moment that you are not a writer, but the franchise owner of Dollar Rent A Car. What are your products? Cars and vans, of course. Now what are your goals? To rent as many vehicles as you can, for as much as you can, and for as long as you can.

Now let's apply these same business characteristics to writing. What are your products? Articles. What are your goals? To sell as many as you can, for as much as you can, and for as long as you can.

Yes, articles, are products. To succeed, you need to make as much money as possible from these products. The more use—in the form of sales—you get out of each product, the more money you will make. This requires that you set your own rates, control the rights that are sold, and expand your market opportunities beyond domestic borders.

As a businessman, my goals has always been to make no less than $4,000 a month—damned good pay for an article writer. To accomplish this, I am required to bring in $1,000 a week. This leads me to the $1-a-word rule (yes, I have rules for just about everything). Quite simply, if a publication is going to pay me $1 a word, that publication is entitled to exclusive rights to my work for a period of one year. Thereafter, all rights automatically revert to me, and I am free to sell the article elsewhere. As with every rule, however, there are exceptions. If, for instance, a publisher wants a work-for-hire arrangement—whereby the publication owns the work forever—my base fee ranges from $1.50 to $2.00 a word.

So, what about the many, many magazines and newspapers that do not have budgets sufficient to pay such rates? Very simply, the rights that a publication receives should be directly proportional to the price paid. I'll even go one step further and say that the rights purchased must never exceed the needs of the publication. An excellent example is the Army Times Publishing Company, based in Virginia. The company's primary market is Department of Defense employees and members of the U.S. military. So, when travel editor Cindi Florit offered me $225 for a feature on Italy's sunken city of Baiae, I gladly accepted. When she asked for all rights, I pulled back the offer and said Army Times could have exclusive rights only in the Department of Defense and U.S. military market, to which she agreed.

The point here is that many editors, it seems, have been trained—primarily because they too began as freelance writers—to believe that all rights or first North American serial rights are theirs for the asking, as long as they have *offered some pittance of compensation. I, for one, would like to know where this absurd thought came from. Army Times Publishing Company had no more need for all rights than does the Prague Post in the Czech Republic.*

This morning, a reader of my Writer On Line column, "Going Global with Mike Sedge" sent a message in which she said: "You suggest that authors establish their own rights, rather than wait and see what an editor offers. It's a concept I've never heard of but find quite compelling and it makes ever so much sense."

Of course it makes sense. It makes good business sense! A major part of guerrilla marketing is not to let the excitement of getting published blur your business vision. That is, you must be fairly compensated for your work and the rights you are selling. The key to rights is that you give each publication what it needs, within the legal boundaries of eth sale. For example, if a newspaper published in New York State is going to publish your article, it has no need for all North American rights. In this same respect, a national publication has no need for world rights. If I am working with a periodical that insists on more rights than are necessary, I immediately up the price of the article accordingly.

Recently, Scientific American Archaeology asked me to write a piece, but insisted on all rights. I realized that they had plans for an international as well as German-language edition of the magazine and, thus, planned to reuse my material. I therefore quoted a price of $1.25 per word, with the agreement that they would take at least two more features. They agreed to the deal. In this case I had sacrificed some standard per-word fee—for all rights usage—in exchange for additional assignments.

Granted, you might lose a sale by doing this. But, in the long run, you will end up making more money by being able to sell your articles again and again. Despite what editors and individuals involved with the New York publishing industry tell you, there are publishers that aggressively resell articles once they have all rights. Buzz magazine goes so far as to advertise the resale of articles. A recent issue, for example, carried an ad reading, among other things, "Reprints of any article are now available from Reprints Management Services. Call today."

Why Freelance Writers Should Become Nonfiction Authors

By Nina Amir

I always wanted to be a writer and make my living getting paid for my words. However, I didn't begin as an author. I began as a magazine journalist, later moving into corporate communication.

Then, one day a friend asked me to edit a book. That event was one of two that changed the trajectory of my career. So, I did. And then I did another and another . . .

The Decision to Become an Author

After a number of years editing books for clients, I began to wonder why *I* wasn't writing books. I entertained the thought of becoming an *author*. I soon learned that I first needed something called a "platform." (A platform is everything you do that creates a fan base or audience in your target market that is ready to buy your book when released.)

I started blogging to promote myself and my forthcoming books. That was the second event that changed the trajectory of my career.

I loved blogging. So, I started another blog and another and another . . .

The popularity of those blogs helped me attract a literary agent. Later, my blogs helped me land a book publishing deal.

How Authorship Changed My Writing Career

Becoming an author changed my writing career in profound ways. It helped me gain:

- More writing work

- More editing work

- More freelance assignments

- Higher pay for writing assignments

It also helped me get more traditional book deals. (I get paid an advance for these books and then royalties on sales.) And it helped me build a larger platform, which means more people read my blogs and buy my traditionally published and self-published books.

If you decide to author a book—even if you self-publish, a whole new world opens up to you. That published book means you know something about writing books. Thus, you can offer your services as a:

- ghostwriter

- book writer

- ebook writer

- booklet writer

You also become an expert on your book topic. This means you get freelance writing assignments on that topic—and command more pay for those assignments.

You also can monetize those assignments in additional ways. Not only can you resell your work to other publications, if you own the rights, you can place articles on the same subject into a print or digital book you publish yourself or a publisher produces for you.

Of course, you can write more books, make more money from those books, and *again* increase the income from your freelance writing business in general, too.

Some writers and journalists don't want to author books. Becoming an author has enhanced everything I do as a freelance writer and journalist. In fact, it's made it more possible for me to make my living by getting paid for my words.

CONCLUSION

How to Overcome the Only Obstacle Between You and a Successful Journalism Career

Our society perpetuates the belief that you must overcome numerous obstacles to succeed. These might include high levels of skill or knowledge, large amounts of time, vast quantities of money, and connections with the right people. While some of this may be true, only one real obstacle blocks the way to your success in any life arena–including writing, publishing, and journalism. If you remove it, the other hurdles become easy to overcome.

Can you identify the obstacle?

You.

You are in your own way. Specifically, your habitual behaviors and mindsets create internal hurdles you must constantly try to jump or remove. These include how you react to situations, your thoughts about circumstances and people, and your beliefs about writing and publishing or becoming a journalist. When you conquer—or change—your habitual habits and mindsets you allow yourself to reach your writing and publishing goals and create your dream career as a writer, journalist, or author.

Personal Growth Makes Writing for Publications Easier

Suppose you ask journalists or freelance writers how they became successful. They likely will say they worked hard, acquired skills and knowledge, and were diligent, committed, and tenacious in pursuing their writing goals. Most also will tell you they "worked on themselves."

In other words, they engaged in some sort of <u>personal growth</u> or development.

<u>High performers</u> know their own behavioral and mental tendencies either slow down or speed up their ability to achieve success. Only if they take time for personal change can they alter those tendencies and succeed professionally or personally.

And so, they invest in themselves by joining masterminds, <u>programs</u>, and courses. They hire therapists and <u>coaches</u>. And they read books about self-improvement and apply what they learn.

These efforts help them change their identity, behavior, and mindset. As a result, achieving success in any life arena becomes much easier.

What Happens When You Get Out of the Way

Here's are two examples demonstrating how getting out of your own way (changing yourself) enhances your ability to succeed.

I had a client who believed he couldn't complete his writing projects. He would describe himself as "someone who never finishes what he starts." That was his identity.

As a result, he found it tough to succeed at anything, including becoming an author. That makes sense since you do need to complete manuscripts (or other writing projects) to become an author.

This man rarely started anything new, including pursuing writing ideas, for fear he would disappoint himself again. His mind was focused on thoughts like, "Why start? I won't finish," or "If I start and don't finish, I'll just feel horrible about myself, so I won't bother." Thus, he looked at his life through that lens (mindset) and only saw incomplete projects.

His behavior followed suit. He didn't start new projects—no matter how important they were to him. He maintained a notebook filled with book ideas, but he never acted on them. And if he did start, he inevitably didn't finish.

Then, he decided to invest in personal development and became one of my coaching clients. He identified a few past book projects he had finished, and realized he could and had completed things previously. He used that knowledge to help him complete current and future projects.

Also, he decided to stop disappointing himself. Instead, he chose to be self-integral and keep his promises to himself. With two new ways of seeing himself—as someone who completes projects and someone who has self-integrity, not only did his mindset shift, but his behaviors, too.

He began thinking, "I finish what I start" and "If I say I will finish something, I do because I have self-integrity." Eventually, these became his beliefs and, therefore, his mindset. He proved that this was true each time he completed a book project or achieved a writing or publishing goal.

So, he began working on writing projects and required himself to finish on a deadline. His new habit was to finish something before starting a new project or goal. As a result, he began consistently finishing the writing projects he started.

As you can imagine, the changes this man made in his mindset and habits made all the difference in his ability to succeed as a writer and author.

Another one of my clients self-published a book on parenting, but she didn't know how—and didn't think she could—monetize her expertise and book with courses or programs. She told me, "I'm not a good businessperson. Plus, I'm horrible with technology." These were her identities, and her habits and mindsets aligned with them perfectly.

She did not approach authorship as a businessperson, and, therefore, rarely promoted her books. Nor did she see authorship from a business perspective; in her mind, she was an artist. And she refused to create an author website, use social media as a promotional tool, or explore ways to coach clients, create courses, or share her knowledge via any type of audio or video tool. She insisted that all these tasks were simply "too techie" for her to try.

Yet, she wanted to support herself. After a few coaching sessions, she admitted that she hadn't known how to write or publish a book, but she figured it out and did so successfully. Therefore, she was someone with the ability to figure things out. That identity served her well as she explored the business side of her chosen career and the technology that would allow her to monetize her book. As a result of adopting this identity, she enrolled in a program that taught her how to create and promote courses.

She also chose to be someone willing to tackle new and difficult tasks. "I'll honor the challenge," she told me. And this new identity allowed her to learn how to use social media and do all the things she learned in the online-course building program in which she invested.

Her mindset and habits aligned with her two new identities—"I am someone with the ability to figure things out" and "I am someone who honors a challenge," which made it much easier for her to do what was necessary to become an author and authorpreneur. In fact, less than a year later, she launched a membership program for parents that featured prerecorded video lessons coupled with live virtual coaching sessions. She also marketed it on social media, and now she earns enough per month to pay her mortgage.

That's the power of doing personal growth work. You stop being the obstacle to your success and, instead, become a person who can do the things necessary to create the success you desire.

Your Habitual Behaviors

Unhelpful habitual behaviors take many forms. For example, you might react with anger whenever someone cuts you off in traffic, hit the snooze button daily when the morning alarm rings, or spend too much time scrolling on social media (rather than writing or pitching publications). Or, like my clients, you might habitually start writing projects you don't finish or say you can't do something because you aren't "that type of person." These habits don't help you succeed.

Not only that, but they are also reactions rather than responses. Reactions are habitual or unconscious ways of behaving in certain situations. Often, something triggers you—like the jerk who cut you off or the sound of the morning alarm—and you react in the same way as always.

On the other hand, responses are intentional and conscious. For example, you decide how to behave when someone cuts you off, like taking a deep breath and feeling grateful that you didn't get in an accident. Or you choose to get out of bed when the alarm rings, so you have time to work on a query letter or article assignment before you must go to work or get the kids off to school.

Reactions reap negative results. They don't help you progress toward success—and sometimes even cause you to move backward a few steps. Responses have a higher probability of positive results because you choose them intentionally to achieve a goal. Therefore, they successfully help you get from Point A to Point B, like from aspiring journalist to published journalist.

Your Habitual Mindsets

Unhelpful habitual mindsets are created by unsupportive thoughts you think repeatedly. If you think a thought often enough, it becomes a belief. And all your beliefs influence your mindset.

Many of your repetitive thoughts stem from early programming or life experiences. For instance, someone influential—like a parent, teacher, or coach—told you something, and you chose to believe it. They "programmed" you to think you were intelligent, stupid, talented, untalented, good at writing, bad at writing, for instance.

Or you had an experience, like being rejected by a magazine editor. You choose to interpret that event to mean something specific. Maybe you decided you are someone who doesn't have salable ideas, isn't a good enough writer, or doesn't have the credentials to get published.

Such thoughts become your beliefs and then, your mindset. And your mindset is the lens through which you see the world, including your experiences and the people you meet.

Let's say you have published 50 or more articles in magazines. Yet, most of your life, you believed you weren't a good writer. When you look at your clip file, you see the articles but still think, "I'm not a good enough writer. After all, I haven't published a book, and good writers are authors. And I haven't been published in a national magazine; great journalists land those types of gigs." Your mindset clouds your vision and doesn't allow you to acknowledge that you are a good and accomplished writer. Thus, you'll never feel confident about your writing.

However, if you believe you are a good writer—and are grateful for the publications that featured your work—you see yourself and your circumstances differently. Your mindset provides a lens that helps you see your worth and value as a writer. And that mindset helps you act in ways that make you successful…including achieving your goal of becoming an author or having your work published in national magazines.

Or let's say life experiences have caused you to believe you aren't good enough. You see everything through this lens. You won't think you are good enough to attract a magazine assignment or book publishing deal. In fact, you'll never feel good enough for anything in the writing and publishing world or in any other life arena.

A not-good-enough mindset is an obstacle to success. It keeps you stuck wondering if you are good enough to tackle any challenge successfully—including landing an article assignment, literary agent, or book deal.

Change your mindset, though, and your ability to achieve successful authorship or a journalistic career change. When you are good enough, you have the confidence to query editors and agents and send a book proposal to a publisher. You have the confidence to do whatever it takes to become a successful, well-paid writer. In fact, you'll know you are good enough to pursue your craziest writing, publishing, and journalism dream. You'll see yourself differently, and your results will be different.

The same holds true when you change any thoughts or beliefs related to becoming a professional writer. Rid yourself of all the negative mental chatter, like "I can't do it," "I'm not techie," "I'm too old," or "I am overwhelmed." Replace those thoughts and beliefs with positive ones, and you will form more positive and supportive habits. You'll also see yourself and the world from a totally different perspective—one that helps you become a writer and journalist.

How to Remove the One Obstacle to Success

Removing the obstacle—you—involves changing your habitual behaviors and mindsets. You accomplish this by becoming intentional and aware of your actions and thoughts. Habits tend to be unconscious. Thus, you must bring them into your consciousness.

Do this by identifying two life arenas first:

- an area in which you feel successful.

- an area in which you feel challenged.

Next, write down the thoughts and behaviors you have related to each.

For example, maybe you feel challenged in the life arena of business. Thus, you might think you don't have the skills or knowledge to monetize your articles by negotiating pay and rights. As a result, you no longer negotiate assignments and rarely pitch previously published work to additional publications. Or you've stopped writing and pitching at all.

Perhaps you feel successful as a parent. You might think, "I'm a good parent," or "Parenting comes naturally to me." As a result, you do whatever it takes to care for your children without hesitation. You make decisions about their well-being and find solutions to parenting problems without doubt regarding your ability to "get it right."

Notice that, in the areas where you succeed, you have positive thoughts and well-planned or confident responses. In the areas you feel challenged, you have negative thoughts, unplanned reactions, or lack of confidence.

Once you have gone through this exercise, your next step involves applying your "success strategies" to the areas where you find it harder to succeed. These are the behaviors and mindsets that help you succeed. For instance, your confidence as a parent could be applied to your writing challenges.

Or you can write new positive thoughts or affirmations to repeat consciously to yourself. Also, decide how to act or respond, choosing ways you feel will result in success.

Three Essentials Necessary for Getting Out of Your Way

Getting out of your own way isn't really that hard. It just takes three essential things:

1. *The willingness to take responsibility for your current behaviors and mindsets.* Once you have done that, you can also be responsible for changing the ones that don't serve you.

2. *Awareness of your behaviors and mindsets.* When you know what you are thinking and doing that makes you an obstacle, you can change them. This moves you out of the way.

3. *The determination to succeed.* As with any endeavor, determination is essential. To successfully remove the obstacle blocking your success, you must be committed to making personal changes that help you succeed.

There is no reason to overcome many hurdles on your way to success as a writer. Instead, overcome the one obstacle blocking your path. When you do that, all the other hurdles disappear or become easy to overcome.

ABOUT NINA AMIR

Nina Amir is an international speaker, award-winning blogger and journalist, 19X Amazon bestselling author, Author Coach, Transformational Coach, and one of 1,000 elite Certified High Performance Coaches in the world—the only one working with writers. Known as the Inspiration to Creation Coach, she helps people combine their purpose and passion, so they get inspired to action and Achieve More Inspired Results.

The author of *How to Blog a Book, The Author Training Manual, and Creative Visualization for Writers*, Amir also has authored 19 e-books, including: *Authorpreneur: How to Build a Business Around Your Book, The Nonfiction Book Proposal Demystified,* and the *Write Nonfiction NOW!* series of six guides. She has had as many as six books on the same Amazon Top 100 list (Authorship) at the same time. Her forthcoming traditionally published book is on writing for change.

To further support writers, Nina founded the Nonfiction Writers' University, Write Nonfiction in November Challenge, and Author of Change Transformational Programs. She also created the Inspired Creator Community, which provides group Transformational (spiritual and personal growth) Coaching to writers and non-writers.

In 2015, Amir received a Certified High Performance Coach (CHPC') certification from the High Performance Institute, which was founded by *New York Times* bestselling author Brendon Burchard. She uses this to coach a variety of clients including writers.

Amir also offers personal development tools at NinaAmir.com and often teaches workshops, teleseminars, and webinars on how to become an author and achieve potential. She speaks to writing groups and at personal growth summits and conferences internationally. She has been on the board of the BEA Bloggers event and the National Association of Independent Writers and Editors.

Amir blogs at How to Blog a Book, Write Nonfiction NOW!, and As the Spirit Moves Me. She was a regular contributor to Thebookdesigner. com and Thefutureofink.com. She has also been the national Jewish Issue Examiner and the National Self-Improvement Examiner at

Examiner.com and had a column on VibantNation.com.

Previously, Amir served as the writing and publishing expert on the popular *Dresser after Dark* radio show. For two years she was a featured expert on *Conversations with Mrs. Claus*, a podcast listened to by 130,000 people in 90 countries each month.

Amir earned a Bachelor of Arts degree in Magazine Journalism with a concentration in psychology from Syracuse University's S.I. Newhouse School of Public Communications. She has edited or written for more than 45 magazines, newspapers, e-zines, and newsletters and produced hundreds of articles in the process. She has interviewed such well-known figures as Usher, Deepak Chopra, Pete Seeger, and Michael Harner. Her essays have been published in five anthologies and appeared in numerous e-zines and Internet article directories. She also has produced hundreds of guest blog posts for well-known sites, and her work has appeared in such books as *Spiritual Pregnancy* and the fifth edition of *How to Write a Book Proposal*.

Amir also has a proven track record as a nonfiction book editor. One of her client's books, *Enlightened Leadership*, was self-published and then purchased and re-released verbatim by Simon & Schuster; it sold over 320,000 copies. Another, *Radical Forgiveness*, won the Writer's Digest Self-Published Book Award (Inspirational category), received a contract from William Morrow but remained self-published and went on to sell 115,000+ copies; much later Sounds True purchased the book.

Born and raised in New York, Amir has traveled extensively around the world. She resides in Placitas, NM, with her husband. It is her passion to help writers remove blocks to success, stay inspired and motivated, and achieve impact with their work.

NINAAMIR
INSPIRATION TO *Creation* COACH

To learn more about Nina and the courses, programs, and coaching she offers, visit www.ninaamir.com.

ABOUT THE AUTHORS

Linda Formichelli is a semi-retired freelance writer. She spent 25 years writing for top publications and businesses, from *Prevention* and *Inc.* magazines to Best Buy and Intel. She's the author or co-author of a dozen books, both self-published and traditionally published, including *The Renegade Writer: A Totally Unconventional Guide to Freelance Writing Success* and *From Pitch to Published: How to Sell Your Article Ideas to Magazines*.

Kelly James-Enger is the author of *Dollars and Deadlines: Make Money Writing Articles for Print and Online Markets*, a book for brand-new freelancers which walks you through 10 actual articles for different markets; how they were pitched, researched, and written; and includes advice on contracts and building your business from scratch. *Six-Figure Freelancing: The Writer's Guide to Making More Money, Second Edition* is a freelancing classic that helps both new and experienced writers boost their bottom line. *Goodbye Byline, Hello Big Bucks: Make Money Ghostwriting Books, Articles, Blogs and More, Second Edition*, shows writers how to break into the ghostwriting/content marketing field.

Seth Mendelson was the publisher and editorial director of Macfadden Communications, overseeing multiple titles across many key categories. Seth has been a journalist since graduating from Syracuse University in 1980. He was a sportswriter and newswriter for Gannett Newspapers, before becoming an editor at Mass Market Retailers, Nonfoods Merchandising and Supermarket Business. Also, Seth was previously editor in chief of Retail Merchandiser. He has been quoted in a number of publications, including *The Wall Street Journal, The New York Times* and many regional newspapers. He currently is semi-retired and writes and edits for West Point's *Black Knight Nation* and the Associated Press.

Zachary Petit (<u>zacharypetit.com</u>) is a design/arts/travel journalist; editor; copywriter; and contributing writer for *Fast Company*. Formerly, he was the editor of the National Magazine Award–winning publication *Print*, the senior managing editor of *HOW* magazine, the longtime managing editor of *Writer's Digest* magazine, and executive editor of several related newsstand titles. Alongside the thousands of articles he has penned as a staff writer and editor, covering everything from the secret lives of mall Santas to creative legends, his words regularly appear in *National Geographic Kids*, and have also popped up in the pages of *National Geographic*, Melissa Rossi's *What Every American Should Know* book series, *McSweeney's Internet Tendency*, and many other outlets. He is the author of *The Essential Guide to Freelance Writing: How to Write, Work and Thrive On Your Own Terms*.

Writer's Relief (WritersRelief.com) is a highly recommended author's submission service that assist writers with preparing their submissions and researching the best markets. They have a service for every budget, as well as a free e-publication for writers, *Submit Write Now!*

Michael Sedge is an American journalist, author, marketing specialist, and entrepreneur. He founded the marketing company Strawberry Media and co-founded the U.S. small business, Michael-Bruno, LLC, which offers architectural design, engineering services, and construction management to the U.S. government in Europe, Africa, and the Middle East. His non-fiction book, *The Lost Ships of Pisa*, won the President of the Italian Republic's Book of the Year Award for a Foreign Author and the "Rusticcello di Pisa" International Journalism Award from the city of Pisa. Worldwide, Sedge is credited in more than 4,000 articles, several audio tape scripts, children's plays, some 30 books (combined collaborations as well as solely authored), and four television documentaries. He is proud of the *Dolce Vita Writers' Holiday*, which he conducted in Tuscany for several years.

Jill Wolfson is the editor of Bay Area Parent. She has worked as a journalist for newspapers and magazines around the country, such as the Fort Lauderdale (Florida) *Sun-Sentinel* and San Jose (California) *Mercury News*. Her award-winning novels for young people include *What I Call Life*; *Home, and Other Big, Fat Lies*; *Cold Hands, Warm Heart*, and *Furious*, all published by Henry Holt. Jill has taught writing at several universities and is a long-time volunteer in a writing program for incarcerated teens.

ACKNOWLEDGEMENTS

Portions of "How to Earn More and Work Less by Managing Your Rights" are reprinted from *Marketing Strategies for Writers* by permission of Allworth Press and the author. Copyright © 1999 Michael Sedge.

Many of the chapters in this ebook first appeared on the Write Nonfiction NOW! blog and are reprinted in this book with permission.

MORE FROM NINA AMIR

The Nonfiction Writers' University

The Nonfiction Writers' University couples comprehensive nonfiction educational resources with group Author Coaching. Members receive the Author Training 101-104 course, a seven-year archive of interviews with writing and publishing experts, e-book writing guides, short courses, and monthly group coaching sessions, during which they get their questions answered and receive support on challenges encountered on the path to nonfiction authorship. This is a one-stop shop for learning to create a successful career as a nonfiction writer and author. Learn more at nonfictionwritersuniversity.com.

The Inspired Creator Community

The Inspired Creator Community offers a unique personal and spiritual growth curriculum and group Transformational Coaching program for those who want to learn how create what matters to them in a spiritually guided manner. Members learn how to be people who can take the actions necessary to create what they desire. By changing from the inside out, they become powerful creators who follow their intuition and inspiration and live lives that feed their souls. Learn more at inspiredcreatorcommunity.com.

Discover more of Nina Amir's courses for nonfiction writers
https://writenonfictionnow.com/courses/

For information on Nina Amir's writing and editing services
https://ninaamir.com/writing-services/

The Write Nonfiction NOW! Guides

Write Nonfiction NOW! Guides are edited by Nina Amir, the founder of the Write Nonfiction in November Challenge, the Nonfiction Writers' University and the Write Nonfiction NOW! blog. They include tips from bestselling authors, seasoned writing coaches, and those who have successfully taken the Write Nonfiction in November Challenge. Each guide teaches a unique aspect of becoming a successful nonfiction author. These guides inform and motivate authors, businesspeople, and even non-writers to use their purpose and passion to create desirable and publishable products.

Click the following links to check out guides to:

- Writing a Book in 30 Days
- Creativity and Flow
- Building Author Platform
- Virtual Book Tours
- A Writing Habit

To find more books by Nina Amir, go to www.booksbyninaamir.com.

PSC PURE SPIRIT CREATIONS